Hand Dug Wells and Their Construction

S. B. Watt & W. E. Wood

ITDG
PUBLISHING

Published by ITDG Publishing
103–105 Southampton Row, London WC1B 4HL, UK
www.itdgpublishing.org.uk

© ITDG Publishing 1977, 1979

First published in 1977
Second edition with new appendix April 1979
Reprinted 1981, 1985, 1990, 1992, 1995, 1998, 2001, 2003

ISBN 0 903031 27 2

A catalogue record for this book is available from the British Library.

ITDG Publishing is the publishing arm of the Intermediate Technology Development Group. Our mission is to build the skills and capacity of people in developing countries through the dissemination of information in all forms, enabling them to improve the quality of their lives and that of future generations.

Printed in Great Britain by Russell Press, Nottingham NG6 0BT

ACKNOWLEDGEMENT

The original publication of this book was made possible by grants from Miss J. Elliott-Binns and from the priest and people of Our Lady and St Oswin's R.C. Parish, Tynemouth, England. The Intermediate Technology Development Group gratefully acknowledges their generosity.

Thanks are also due to Oxfam and to Peace Corps (USA) for their kind permission to reproduce many photographs from their libraries; and a special thanks to Christine Marsden for her invaluable help with the typing.

CONTENTS

LIST OF PHOTOGRAPHS

PREFACE

At least 1000 million people in the world lack adequate access to a safe supply of drinking water. At present this number is growing faster than the rate at which new and improved supplies are being constructed. We face the very real prospect of an ever-worsening situation with each year seeing more and more people without the basic human need of a safe drinking water supply. The solutions to this grave problem are not exclusively technical. Great progress in the social, economic, institutional and manpower fields must be made before any major counter-offensive can be launched. However, there are also very real technical challenges to be faced. These are of two kinds. Firstly it is necessary to develop, test and apply new technologies to do jobs for which existing technologies are not suited. Secondly, it is necessary to sift the huge range of existing technology in order to select those items which are truly appropriate to developing countries and then to make these technologies available as widely, as quickly and as cheaply as possible. Part of this second task involves the publication of simple and easily digested material to bring information concerning appropriate technologies to the widest audience. This book is a major contribution to this endeavour. For many people of the world, relatively shallow ground-water sources represent the cheapest and most readily available supplies of potable water. This book presents simply, but in detail, a range of technology suitable for exploiting these ground-water sources at low cost, with minimum sophisticated technology and with the greatest input of village labour and skills. The authors are to be congratulated on writing a book which, I feel certain, will become the standard reference source on the construction of hand dug wells.

Richard Feachem
Ross Institute of Tropical Hygiene

PREFACE TO THE SECOND EDITION

This edition has been expanded by the inclusion of an appendix on the use of explosives in well-sinking work.

The appendix is intended to describe the use of explosives for sinking large diameter wells through hard rocks. The information given in this appendix is not adequate to instruct an inexperienced person. It should be used as a practical guide for those already experienced and qualified in the use of explosives. *It is not intended to instruct or qualify an inexperienced person in rock-blasting work.*

The supplement describes the various methods of using explosives in well-sinking work, and recommends that the burning fuse type of detonation be used because of its simplicity and foolproof nature. Electric detonation is described and the safety rules that must be observed if accidents are to be avoided are also included.

S B Watt
W E Wood

INTRODUCTION

This manual is intended as a guide to the hand digging of wells, especially village wells in tropical or sub-tropical areas, where cost has to be kept to a minimum and the villagers themselves are able and willing to contribute the labour required.

The methods described combine traditional principles with modern techniques. Well sinking is an ancient craft going back thousands of years, but in the past many of the so-called wells upon which villagers have had to rely for their water supply consisted merely of unlined and unprotected holes into which children, animals or refuse could fall, liable to collapse on to the sinkers or under the users, and a constant danger to health due to the polluted condition of the water supplied. By contrast the present day well is permanent, safe and hygienic, an asset to the village, and a contributory factor in improving the health and well-being of its inhabitants.

The manual describes hand-dug shaft wells and their construction by relatively unskilled villagers. Modern concepts, methods and designs are incorporated, but in such a way that those who will carry out the actual work do not require a high degree of education. training or supervision. Much of the equipment can be made locally and costs (especially the cost of imported materials) can be kept to a minimum. The simple directions are based upon proven methods and satisfactory results gathered from various parts of the world. Wells constructed by the methods indicated need be in no way inferior to those produced by mechanical equipment at many times the expense. They can be as reliable, as versatile, as adaptable to varying conditions and they can yield as much water of as high a quality, even though they may not be capable of being constructed so quickly.

Hand dug wells are used for a variety of purposes and their

design may vary accordingly. They are widely used for irrigation, in which case the health precautions called for in domestic wells will be unnecessary, but provision will be required for equipment to extract the larger quantities of water -- such contrivances as windmills, shadufs or animal driven 'Persian wheels' are often fitted. Similar devices are also fitted when wells are to be used for stock watering. The most common use, however, and the one principally envisaged throughout this manual, is to supply drinking and domestic water to small communities.

In the first part some general principles are briefly described together with a reference to the health implications of a hygienic source of water and some notes on the organisation and preparation of well sinking work. Part II describes in simple detail the actual construction of a particular size and type of well that has proved successful in many parts of the world under widely differing conditions. This part has been written to be complete in itself — a practical guide to those actually engaged in well construction. Part III deals with alternative materials and techniques which may be more suitable in certain circumstances. Part IV describes in greater detail the standard equipment and materials used, and Part V comprises additional information that may be of use to those interested in well sinking.

It is hoped that the whole will serve as a guide to those wishing to encourage villagers to improve the reliability and wholesomeness of their drinking water. The authors are convinced that there is no single measure that can, at such a small outlay, so raise the standard of health, comfort, social and economic well-being of small communities everywhere.

S B Watt
W E Wood

PART I   PRINCIPLES OF WELL DIGGING

CHAPTER 1 GROUNDWATER OCCURRENCE

A well is a device for extracting water from the ground. Before considering the well itself we should know something of the nature, occurrence and behaviour of the groundwater to be extracted.

At all times, and all over the world, there is taking place a movement of water in its various forms. We call this the hydrological cycle and very briefly it works like this: the energy from the sun's rays evaporates water from the sea, from open water on land and from the leaves of vegetation. The water vapour thus formed rises and collects into clouds, which are carried by the wind to the point where meteorological conditions cause them to precipitate as rain or snow — the place where this precipitation takes place may be near the point of evaporation or hundreds of miles away. When the rain falls over land, part soaks into the ground and part runs off in streams or rivers to return eventually to the sea. Of the water that soaks into the ground, part is used by vegetation and part sinks below root level through porous soil until it reaches bedrock or other impermeable layer. Then, under the force of gravity, it gradually finds its way downhill until it either emerges as springs or returns below ground to the sea to be re-evaporated in due course.

The part of the hydrological cycle in which the well-sinker is especially interested is that between the water first sinking into the ground and its re-emergence in spring, river or the sea itself. At this stage it is known as 'groundwater' and the saturated soil layer containing it is called an 'aquifer'. Aquifers may be of several types; where the lower part of a porous soil that reaches to the surface is saturated, it is known as an 'open' aquifer, the upper surface of the water it contains being called the 'water table'. This is the unpumped water level found in a well. It is open aquifers of this sort that are most frequently tapped by hand dug wells.

Sometimes an aquifer is overlain by an impermeable layer

15

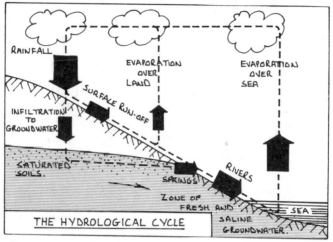

THE HYDROLOGICAL CYCLE

of soil or rock, in which case the contained water may be under pressure. In wells sunk into strata of this nature the water will rise above the point at which it is encountered, sometimes even reaching the surface of the ground. Such wells are called 'artesian' (if the water rises to the surface) or 'subartesian' (if it rises part of the way).

In other cases the descending water may be held above a relatively small area of impervious rock to form a 'perched' aquifer. Since the quantity of water held depends on the area of the impervious layer, wells sunk into perched aquifers are liable to exhaust their capacity and dry up if too much water is drawn from them.

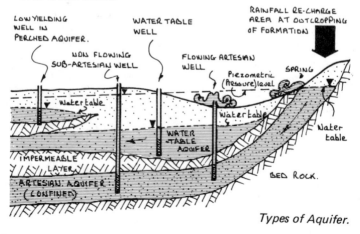

Types of Aquifer.

The natural pressure of water in an artesian aquifer remains fairly constant throughout the year, but the water table of an open aquifer will fluctuate, rising to its highest level after the rains and falling during the dry season. This is a most important point to be considered if a well sunk into such an aquifer is to give a reliable yield throughout the year.

The amount of water stored in an open aquifer, and hence the level of its water table, will materially depend on the quantity of rainfall entering the ground in the vicinity and on the geological nature of the soil of which it is composed. The fraction of rainfall that soaks in to feed the underground storage will depend largely on the composition and form of the land surface; steep, hard areas will shed most of the water that falls on them, whereas flat, sandy and vegetated areas will permit a larger proportion of the rain to penetrate. It is thus possible, by slowing down the rate of surface run-off, to increase the amount that enters the soil. This may be achieved by a combination of such measures as contour ploughing, terracing steep slopes, bunding flood plains and building small dams across the head waters of streams — these measures will also be valuable in helping to control soil erosion.

In those dry parts of the world where the greater part of the year's rainfall occurs in sudden storms, building cheap, shallow dams or bunds across flood wadis is of particular value. These will slow down the rate of flow, allowing flash floods time to soak down and be stored in the sandy layers at the bottom of the wadi. The saturated top soil will allow a strong crop to grow after the flood has passed, and the stored water below can be pumped up for use later in the year.

The amount of ground water that is stored in an aquifer and can be extracted from it depends on the material of which the soil is composed. A good aquifer must be able to store water between its grains or in its fissures, and must also permit the stored water to flow into the well. The 'porosity' of an aquifer is a measure of its ability to store water; its 'permeability' is its property of permitting the through-flow of water. Some silts and most clays are able to store quite large volumes of water and yet are relatively useless as aquifers because they will not readily yield it into a well. In a good aquifer the pores are both large enough to hold ground water and sufficiently interconnected to allow it to flow freely.

Some aquifers extend over many hundreds of square kilometres with little variation in characteristics. Once such an area has been identified the performance of a well within its boundaries can be predicted with reasonable accuracy and a well construction programme can be planned with confidence. Other aquifers may vary in character over short distances, making the potential yield of a well very difficult to predict.

Tapping groundwater

To take water from an aquifer, a hole is dug into the saturated material and is then lined to prevent collapse of its sides. Either the side lining or the bottom must be porous, and this part of the well is called the 'intake'. Water from the aquifer will flow through the intake until the level of the water surface within the well coincides with the surrounding water table, when the natural flow will stop.

As soon as water is extracted from the well by bucket or pump the level inside will fall causing a difference between

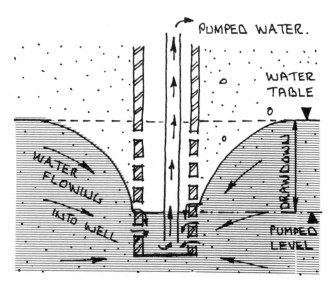

Drawdown in a pumped well.

the internal and external water pressures and hence an inward flow through the intake. This flow must not be so fast that the sand or other aquifer material is carried into the well, but the quantity entering must be sufficient to equal the amount withdrawn. If the intake has been correctly designed and the withdrawal is steady, a balance will be reached with the water level within the well being some distance below the water table, this distance being known as the 'draw-down'.

Deepening the well will usually increase the supply of water available from the well as the greater draw-down causes water to flow in from the aquifer at a faster rate. Making the well of greater diameter increases the area of the intake through which the water can flow:—

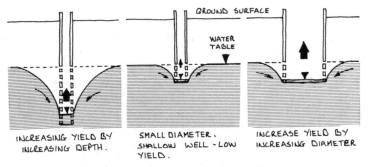

Increasing the yield of a well.

In most cases, increasing the depth is a more certain way of improving yield than enlarging the diameter, though, as will be shown, there are limits to the extent to which this can be done using hand digging methods.

When a number of wells are sited close together, pumping large quantities from one may affect the output of others nearby; if the total extracted from all the wells is in excess of the capacity of the aquifer, its underground storage will be depleted and the water table throughout the area will drop. This is not likely to happen, however, with the type of well under consideration in this manual.

Components of a hand dug well

After the water has entered the well through the intake it must be raised to the surface and then extracted for use. It is

19

convenient to consider any well as consisting of three components — the intake, the shaft and the wellhead. When a well is dug by hand the shaft is the first component constructed, since this provides the access to the aquifer enabling the intake to be inserted in place. The wellhead is the final stage; its design will depend on the method of extraction to be used (e.g. pump, buckets or other water lifting devices).

The purpose of the intake is to support the exposed section of the aquifer and to permit water to flow in while excluding solids that might enter with the water. In some geological conditions (e.g. in sandstone or fissured rock) it may be possible to dispense with this component, but in the more usual cases where the aquifer is of sand or gravel the intake may be considered the key to the future performance of the well. The intake is usually built telescoped and 'floating' inside the shaft lining; this prevents the cracking or collapse of the shaft lining if the intake settles.

The shaft is for access during construction and after completion it serves to retain the sides in place, to prevent the ingress of water from near the surface (which 'shallow' water may be contaminated and unsafe) and to act as a foundation for the wellhead. It must therefore be lined with strong and waterproof material. Unlined wells have in the past been responsible for accidental deaths, both of the sinkers (during construction) and of the users (after completion) through collapse or caving. Water from unlined and unprotected wells can become infested with parasites or contaminated with disease-causing bacteria; even when a well is sunk through sound self-supporting rock, the top three metres or so must be made waterproof to exclude this hazard.

Ideally every well should be fitted with a sealed wellhead that will prevent insects, windblown dust, animals or refuse from entering the shaft. Such a wellhead calls for a pump (hand-, wind,- or mechanically-operated) which, if properly fitted, enables the well to remain completely hygienic throughout its life. If for financial or other reasons it is not possible to fit a pump the wellhead must be designed to reduce chances of contamination to a minimum.

Methods of self-help well construction

The present manual deals in detail with one particular

method of self-help well sinking — the hand dug well in which the shaft is of sufficient size to enable the sinkers to descend and work below ground. It is worth noting that there is another type of well in which all the construction is carried out on the surface, from which a tube is drilled, jetted, driven or otherwise forced downward until the aquifer is reached, after which a pump is fitted to the upper end of the tube. (A separate manual is under preparation which deals with the different techniques involved.)

Each method has its advantages under differing circumstances. The tube well, for instance, is especially suitable where plenty of water exists in aquifers a short distance below ground level, such as may often be found alongside rivers or lakes. When powered mechanical drilling equipment is available it is possible to sink boreholes to greater depths than can be penetrated by hand methods, and also to drill through hard rock that would present serious difficulties to the sinkers of a hand dug well.

However, the method described in this book is of wide application, has been used in many parts of the world under differing conditions, is easily taught to relatively unskilled workers, requires the minimum of expensive imported materials and equipment, and produces sufficient water for a village or small community provided that the aquifer to be tapped is suitable. It also utilises traditional well-sinking skills, adapting them to incorporate modern techniques and materials. At the same time the experience gained by villagers in the construction of their well may be put to good use later in connection with other self-help projects. Another very important reason for choosing the hand dug well is that simple but bulky water lifting devices, such as the ubiquitous rope and bucket, can be used; mechanical hand pumps that are needed for surface constructed tube wells have a notorious record of failure in rural areas and, if the pump breaks, the well is often abandoned.

Dimensions of hand dug wells

Traditionally, wells have been constructed with either square or circular cross sections, but the advantages of economy and strength in both excavation and lining are so overwhelmingly with the circular shape that this is used for virtually all wells constructed today, with the exception of short-lived, timber-lined excavations.

The first consideration in well design is, therefore, the diameter. Neglecting for the moment those very large wells built for special purposes, the diameter chosen normally represents a compromise between economic and practical considerations. It can be shown that the cost of a lined well varies almost exactly with its diameter, taking into account the larger volume of excavation and the increased thickness of lining necessary in a larger well. The smallest practical internal diameter is governed by the room needed for one or two men to work inside; experience shows that about 1 metre is the minimum for one man and 1.3 metres for two. It has also been found that two men working together achieve more in one day than a single man can manage in two.

Other considerations affecting the size of the shaft include the greater natural ventilation of a larger hole, the more efficient size of lifting buckets and other equipment that can be used during construction, the additional room for concreting operations, the ability to telescope caisson tubes within the lining and still have enough room for a man to work within these tubes. All these arguments favour 1.3 metres as the finished diameter; on the other hand increasing beyond this figure does not appear to give any great advantage.

For these and other reasons the wells described in Part II of this manual have a finished, lined diameter of 1.3 metres. As to depth, wells have been successfully sunk by this method to more than 120 metres, but about half that depth is usually considered to be the limit of practical sinking.

It is worth noting that in some parts of the world, India in particular, wells are excavated with diameters of 10 metres or more to act both as reservoirs for surface run-off during the rainy season and access into the aquifer during the dry. They are very expensive to construct, are wide open to pollution from the surface, cannot easily be sunk to a sufficient depth because of the difficulty of keeping the water level down during excavation. Unless they are sunk into a very permeable aquifer they will not yield much more water than the more normal sized well, but sometimes they may provide useful storage for water seeping from slow flowing aquifers.

22

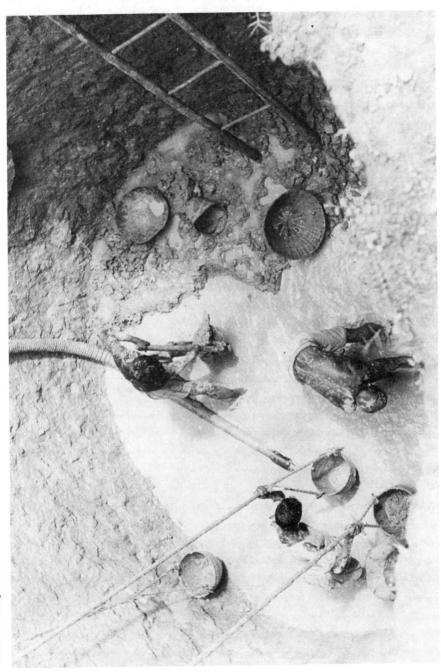

Photo 1   Large Oversize Hand Dug Wells a) Emptying a well of very large diameter is difficult unless a motor powered pump is available. The water is pumped out to allow construction to proceed. — India. (These wells are larger and therefore more expensive than those recommended in this manual and are all liable to pollution.)

Photo 2   Large Oversize Hand Dug Wells b) Masonry lined, 15 metre square well, with steps for access. — India

Photo: Simon Watt

Photo 3   c) Circular, unlined hand dug well, 10 metres in diameter. The well is excavated through stable soils and is used for irrigation. — India.

Photo 4   d) Excavating 10 metre diameter well and removing spoil up a ramp cut into the side of the well. Well excavated into slow flowing acquifer. — India.

Photo: Simon Watt

Photo: Barney Wood

Wells of this kind are not recommended for domestic supplies.

Well construction materials

The component of the well in which most material is used is the lining of the shaft, and it is useful to consider the forces that act upon this lining.

There are two particular types of loading that must be resisted by the wall of the shaft, those acting sideways which can distort or even collapse the shaft, and the vertical forces (either compression or tension) due to the weight of the lining itself which can produce buckling, splitting and caving and may lead to subsidence of the wellhead.

The soils and rocks surrounding the well are not stable; they are always liable to move and settle due to the weight of the soils above. The well lining must be able to withstand the compressive load from all directions exerted by running sand or swelling shales as well as concentrated pressures from shifting rocks or strata:—

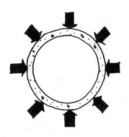

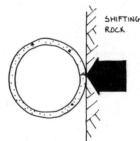

*Uniform loading
from fluid soils.*

*Concentrated loading
from shifting rocks.*

Concentrated loads on one side of the lining will cause it to bend out of shape; if it is not sufficiently flexible it will fracture and collapse or crack and allow contaminated water to enter the well. Provided that the material of which it is composed can adjust itself to the strains imposed, and provided that it is bonded to the wall of the shaft, the lining will distribute the loading around the shaft and remain unfractured. Of all the materials commonly in use for well lining a thin wall of reinforced concrete, cast in-situ in the well, fulfills this condition most satisfactorily.

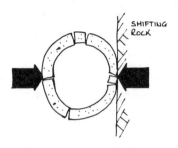
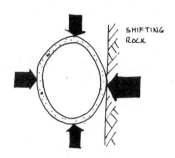

Inflexible lining cracking under point loading.

A thin flexible lining bending and distributing the loading to the soils.

The lining must also be able to withstand the vertical forces acting on it due to its own weight. Most modern wells are lined with reinforced concrete in stages or 'lifts', each lift supporting itself by skin friction against the side of the shaft and by 'curbs' dug into the surrounding soil. Each is then allowed to settle completely before the gaps between them are filled.

In some methods of well construction, such as caisson sinking, no curbs are used and skin friction may be very uneven. As a result a section that is firmly held may crush under the weight of an unsupported upper section, or split if a lower section settles. This latter condition is particularly likely to occur if the aquifer collapses due to solids flowing into the well through over-pumping.

Because of these considerations, and because reinforced concrete is simple to mix and lay, relatively cheap in most places, and adaptable in other ways, it is the material most frequently chosen for well linings. Its use is described in detail in Part II of this manual, while Part III refers to the use of alternative materials which, because of their availability, may be preferred in some cases.

For the intake section porous concrete, i.e. concrete made with cement and gravel but with a very small proportion of sand, is a useful choice where it is intended that the water should enter through the walls. Alternative materials for the intake include normal concrete incorporating 'weep-holes', or a graded gravel filter at the bottom of a waterproof shaft. All these methods are fully described.

Seasonal construction

One of the limitations of hand sinking is the difficulty of penetrating far enough into the aquifer to ensure an adequate depth of water in the well at all times in the future. Below a certain depth the water comes in too fast during construction for the well to be pumped sufficiently dry for the diggers to work efficiently.

This difficulty is made worse by the fact that the water table fluctuates seasonally and may drop considerably at the end of a long dry period. As it is usually not possible to arrange a well sinking programme so that setting of the intakes always coincides with the lowest level of the water table, a well completed during another season and giving a good yield at that time may run dry when the level drops later.

A system known as 'telescoping' has been devised to mini-mise this drawback. In effect this consists of constructing at the lower end of the shaft a second independent length of lining of smaller diameter projecting upward into the shaft. This is left in position until the appropriate season of low water level comes round, when it is only necessary to descend, excavate the material within the smaller diameter tube, and allow this to sink under its own weight until the lower water level is reached:—

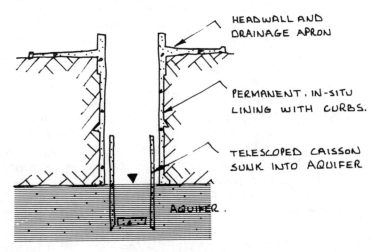

HEADWALL AND DRAINAGE APRON

PERMANENT, IN-SITU LINING WITH CURBS.

TELESCOPED CAISSON SUNK INTO AQUIFER

AQUIFER.

Cross section through well.

CHAPTER 2 HEALTH ASPECTS OF WELL CONSTRUCTION

Water and health

Many of the diseases that cause illness and death to mankind are 'water related' in one way or another. They can be listed under various heads, e.g.:

(a) Water-borne diseases — those that may be carried in water and infect consumers. Cholera, dysentery, typhoid and hepatitis are of this class.

(b) Parasitic diseases, where the organism causing the sickness spends part of its life cycle in an aquatic host, for example guinea worm or bilharzia cercaria. Otherwise known as 'water-based' diseases.

(c) Filth-borne diseases, or diseases of dirt — those whose incidence could be reduced if ample water were available for washing and hygiene. Scabies, tropical ulcers, trachoma and infantile diarrhoea are examples. Sometimes referred to as 'water-washed' diseases.

(d) Water associated diseases, spread by insects that breed in water. Malaria, river blindness and sleeping sickness come under this heading. The mosquito, simulium fly or other causative agent is described as a 'water-related insect vector'.

The first two of these classes can be drastically reduced by providing water that is free from infection. The third class will become less prevalent if sufficient water is available for personal washing and domestic hygiene, so the construction of wells giving ample supplies of safe water will serve to protect the public from all three.

The fourth class of diseases will not be directly affected by well construction, but there may be an indirect effect if villagers no longer have to frequent swamps or other infested spots to collect their water. While it cannot be claimed that the improvement of drinking water will in itself eradicate schistosomiasis this also can be reduced if women and children do not have to enter infested water in order to collect their domestic supplies or to wash clothes.

It must be understood that these remarks apply only to a hygienic well — one that has been designed and constructed in such a way as to protect the water it contains from contamination and that is used and maintained in a hygienic manner. If these conditions are not fulfilled the well itself, instead of being a factor of community health improvement may actually become a means of spreading those very diseases that it was designed to prevent.

Hygiene education is therefore essential if the full benefits of any water supply improvement scheme are to be realised. Unless the local people understand the risks of contaminated water, the need for safe waste disposal, and the importance of personal care they will not appreciate the necessity for protecting the supply.

Most water related diseases are spread by wastes from an infected or ill person being transmitted to the water supply in some way. Man is, unfortunately, the main reservoir of most of the diseases that make him sick, and all water supply improvement schemes should be supplemented by sanitary measures that cut the cycle of disease by the efficient disposal of human wastes. These should include the protection of the water supply from contamination and, where appropriate, the treatment of the water before it is used to destroy any disease-causing bacteria, viruses or parasites:—

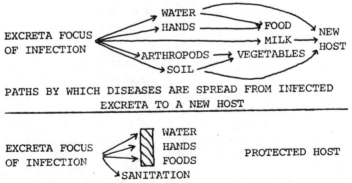

PATHS BY WHICH DISEASES ARE SPREAD FROM INFECTED EXCRETA TO A NEW HOST

STOPPING THE TRANSMISSION OF FAECAL-BORNE DISEASES BY THE EFFICIENT DISPOSAL OF HUMAN WASTES

Prevention of contamination of the well

There are three routes by which the water in a well may become contaminated, through the wellhead, through the lining, or through the water entering the intake.

An open well without a wellhead is always potentially dangerous. The ground around it becomes worn and slopes towards the shaft, allowing rain and spillage to wash into the well. In addition, in areas where guinea worm is endemic, the eggs of this revolting parasite are carried into the water below to transmit the disease to a subsequent user. Hookworm and other infections can flourish in the soil immediately round the shaft, to be picked up by the bare feet of the villagers. If people are allowed to enter the well, to use insanitary

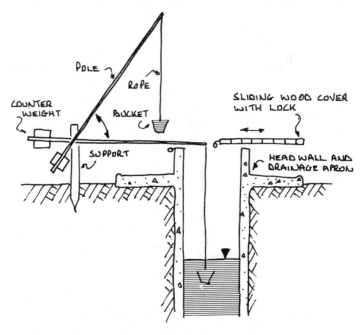

Domestic water supply. Brick lined shallow hand dug well with headwall and drainage apron. Water is lifted out by bucket 'Shaduf' device made from bamboo. The bucket remains suspended above ground between periods of use. A sliding wooden cover which is locked by the well owner prevents rubbish from being thrown into the well. Thailand.

Photo 5   Protected well with sliding cover and Shaduf
water lifting device.

Photo 6 Wellhead Contamination — a) New latrines built alongside a well which will be abandoned. Even if the well is filled in, the aquifer is still liable to be contaminated. — India.

Photo 7 b) 3 metre diameter hand dug well brick lined with a low headwall. Sullage water is tipped by the wellhead — the users carry contamination onto the wall on their feet and this drains down into the well. This well can be improved by constructing a drainage apron and making the headwall too narrow to stand on. — India.

buckets to raise their water, to defecate or to wash themselves or their clothes in the vicinity, or if animals are per-
mitted to approach the open well mouth, a whole new range
of disease-spreading contamination may pollute the well.

A properly designed wellhead can exclude most of these
hazards. Two features are essential — a curb or headwall
rising sufficiently high above ground surface to prevent anything from washing or blowing into the well mouth, and
narrow enough to discourage the users from standing on it,
and an impervious apron 2m wide, sloping away from the
shaft in all directions. This apron should be drained and the
drainage taken to a soakaway a safe distance away.

For complete safety a raised sealed cover is needed, but
such a cover is only feasible where a pump is to be fitted.
Where the well is to be left open for ropes and buckets to be
used to draw the water, precautions must be taken to mini-
mise the hazards of contamination, and some of these are
described later. A moveable cover may be provided to protect
the shaft from wind-blown dust, insects and the like when
the well is not in use:—

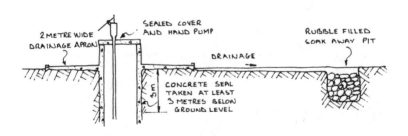

Prevention of wellhead pollution.

Pollution may enter through the shaft lining if this is not
watertight. When a well is sunk through material such as
sandstone, hard laterite or other rock, the walls of the shaft
may be sufficiently strong to stand without support, and in
such cases lining is often omitted. In every case, however, the
top 3 metres at least should be made waterproof by lining to
prevent seepage from the surface soil layers, which are the
most likely to carry dangerous contaminants.

When a well is lined with material other than concrete, e.g.

brickwork, masonry or similar substitute, particular care must be given to ensuring the water tightness of the top 3 metres and its junction with the wellhead.

The water in the aquifer may become polluted before it reaches the intake. A source of pollution, such as a pit privy or animal pen, will produce contaminated water that will soak downwards into the soil. Usually the polluted drainage will become filtered and purified within a short distance as it travels downward, but if the water table is too close to the surface purification may be incomplete before the water enters the intake. A well should therefore be located as far away from potential sources of pollution as possible (certainly no nearer than 50m) and at a higher level of the water table. Obviously the more densely populated the area the more difficult will this be to achieve. It may be possible to arrange for privies in the immediate vicinity to be cleared before well construction starts, but the saturated ground around them may remain hazardous for a long time after their use has been stopped:—

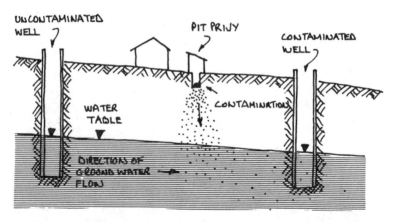

Contaminated wastes from pit privy soaking down to the aquifer and into the well.

One further potential hazard may render the water in a well unpleasant or impossible to drink — a concentration of salts dissolved from the soil by the groundwater in its passage to or within the aquifer. Some of these (e.g. chlorides, sulphates) make the water bitter or unpalatable, some may be

Photo 8 Wellhead Contamination —
c) Hand dug well used for water supply.
The mouth is lined with loose stone
blocks but polluted surface water and
rubbish can enter the well. — Upper
Volta

Photo 9 d) Digging into the bed of
a dry river to reach water. These wells
are particularly liable to gross
contamination. — Ethiopia.

dangerous in excessive concentrations (e.g. heavy metals, nitrates), some constitute a nuisance only (e.g. iron salts that stain clothes washed in the water). All are difficult and expensive to remove. If there is any doubt a sample of the water should be sent for chemical analysis before a well is opened for public use.

Salt concentrations in the ground usually occur over a fairly wide area, and evidence of their presence in nearby wells should always lead to suspicion that any new well may produce water that is not safely potable.

Disinfection and maintenance

On completion a new well should be properly disinfected before use, since it may have been contaminated by the sinkers themselves. The risk can be reduced by simple hygienic precautions during construction; above all, defecation within or in the immediate vicinity of the well must be strictly forbidden. Even so disinfection should always be carried out, and the procedure is described in detail in Part II.

Before a well is handed over for public use it is important that arrangements are made for its future maintenance and hygienic use. Good maintenance depends on the designation of a person responsible for keeping the structure in good order. Hygienic use can only be achieved if those who will be drawing water from the well know the basic rules, appreciate the health implications for themselves and their neighbours, and actually want to keep their water source clean and wholesome. Public opinion must be won; experience has shown that persuasion can achieve results that regulations cannot.

Nevertheless there are certain precautions that can be taken by the village authorities. They should ensure that privies or other sources of contamination are kept at a proper distance from the wellhead, that if animals are to be watered this should be done (preferably from properly constructed troughs) some way from the well and the wellhead should be fenced to keep animal droppings and the beasts themselves clear of the apron, that washing facilities (for people and for their clothes) are provided far enough away to avoid the drainage seeping back into the ground around the wellhead.

Where the well is an open one periodic cleaning should be

arranged. In some parts of the world this is made into a special occasion at the time of the lowest water level, the villagers cooperating in drawing the water in the well to the lowest level possible, while one or two men are lowered into the shaft to remove any accumulation of rubbish, sediment or vegetable growth. After such cleaning the well should again be disinfected (using the same procedure described in Part II) before being put back into use.

Hygienic usage is made easier if the wellhead is designed with this in mind. If a pump (operated by hand or otherwise) is fitted this is easier to achieve, though an important point to watch is that the pump must always be self-priming — contamination can start from dirty water used to prime a hand pump. Where the well is an open one a potential source of pollution is the use of ropes and buckets. This can be minimised if communal ones are provided, so fixed to the wellhead that they cannot be removed, thrown on to the ground, or stored in an insanitary manner. Such devices as windlasses or counterpoised buckets (one at each end of a rope passing over a high pulley) are a fairly good compromise, though there is always some danger from contamination due to handling.

In places where it is customary (and unavoidable) for villagers to have their own ropes and buckets they should be persuaded to hang them up clear of rats and domestic animals when out of use, and to refrain from depositing them on bare ground near the wellhead before and after they are used for drawing water. A type of wellhead designed to avoid this risk as much as possible is described in the manual; it also includes a device to reduce spillage when filling carrying containers from the well buckets.

It should be made the responsibility of some particular individual to see that the surroundings of the well are kept clean and in good repair. The apron should be periodically swept, if a removable wellhead cover is provided it should be placed in position at the end of each day's drawing, any cracks that may appear in the concrete should be made good promptly, incipient erosion around the apron should be remedied (otherwise the concrete itself may become undermined and crack), the drainage channel and soakaway from the apron should be kept clear. Where a pump is fitted (even the simplest of hand pumps) this should be regularly inspected, worn bearings or leaking glands should be promptly attended to so that the need for major repairs is avoided.

The users themselves should have the importance of cleanliness carefully explained to them, and they should understand why it is so necessary for their water source to be kept wholesome and safe. If it is put to them properly in the first place it should be unnecessary to have to try and enforce hygienic practice. They themselves have to be the ones to see that no refuse is ever thrown into the well, that defecation, clothes washing and animal watering do not take place in its vicinity, that children do not play with or damage the pump or rollers. They should appreciate that the well is a community asset — in other words their own property — to be protected by them and their neighbours.

At the same time it is a good thing to explain to them the importance of protecting their domestic water after it has been taken from the well. Disease can be spread within a family through water stored in open pots in the home, especially if these are not protected from domestic animals, rodents or insects. Precautions against the breeding of mosquito larvae in domestic water pots are especially necesary in areas where malaria or yellow fever are prevalent. Filariasis may be spread where spillage or sullage water is allowed to collect into pools and the resulting infection is not confined to the household where the nuisance occurs.

A final point concerns special precautions to be taken whenever there is a particular health hazard such as an epidemic of cholera or typhoid in the neighbourhood. In cases like this it is wise to add a mild but continuous dose of disinfectant to the water in the well; various simple devices can be used for this purpose, one of the more usual being the lowering into the well of a sealed but porous pot containing chloride of lime. Such a pot can give protection for two or three weeks without the concentration of chlorine in the water ever rising to an unpalatable degree.

CHAPTER 3 SELF-HELP WELL CONSTRUCTION PROJECTS

Digging a well by hand is a 'labour-intensive' activity; in other words the manual effort put in represents a large proportion of the total cost of the project. By contrast a drilled borehole using mechanical equipment, steel casing and other imported items but requiring only two or three men for a short time to install it, is 'capital-intensive' because labour costs constitute a small percentage of the total.

Consequently hand digging is a particularly appropriate method of well construction in low income village communities where the people themselves can lend a hand on the construction but would find it difficult to contribute cash on the same scale. There are additional advantages; the villagers take a more proprietorial attitude toward a well that they have helped to build and so are more likely to keep it clean and in good repair. Some of the skills, such as the mixing and placing of concrete learnt during well construction can be put to good use by them on other self-help projects unconnected with well sinking. A trained well team can duplicate the work elsewhere and can also carry out improvements (such as well deepening) using the same techniques.

However, the building of a sanitary well requires preparation, organisation and some expenditure on equipment and materials. In addition to the preparatory work described in the next chapter, the well sinkers have to be recruited, trained and equipped with tools. Until they are sufficiently experienced to operate on their own they must be supervised. Apart from the possibility of the well being a failure there are personal dangers to the sinkers against which precautions must be taken. Sand and gravel or other aggregate for R.C. lined wells must be collected and transported to the site in good time for use as required. Cement and reinforcing rods must be purchased, brought to the site and protected against theft or weather damage.

To a great extent the organisation of a well sinking project depends on whether a single well is to be dug or whether a number are being considered. In many ways a well is more difficult and expensive when it is the only one to be constructed than when it forms part of a larger programme. Tools and equipment purchased or made locally are just as necessary for one well as for several but when their expense is spread over a number of projects the cost per well of this item is obviously reduced accordingly. In this manual a number of make-shift devices are described which enable equipment costs for a single well to be cut to the minimum but this can only be done with some loss of efficiency.

Unless trained well sinkers are available, the first well sunk will require a great deal more supervision than subsequent ones while the sinkers are gaining experience. Even so the efficiency and quality of the work will improve as more wells are sunk, while wastage of effort and materials should correspondingly reduce. There is much to be said therefore for planning well digging as part of a programme but the methods described in this manual are applicable both to single and to multiple projects.

For really large programmes where, say, several hundred wells are to be sunk there are a number of more expensive items of equipment that can improve efficiency and cut costs. Such items include mechanical pumps, ventilating fans, compressed air winches, drills, explosives, orange-peel grabs, concrete mixers and vibrators. These are outside the scope of this manual which is intended for use by those engaged in more modest self-help programmes.

The actual construction of the well is carried out by a team of six men under a 'foreman' or 'headman'. (Where the proper equipment is not available this number may have to be increased to seven or eight.) Two of these are 'sinkers', who will work down the well shaft; it is an advantage if these men have had previous experience of operating below ground, even if only as 'traditional' well sinkers. The remainder work above ground on concrete mixing, on disposing of excavated material and on hoisting gear for raising and lowering men and materials. As a rough guide the team will be employed for about twice the number of working days that the well is deep (in metres), plus a week to complete the wellhead and another week on site clearance.

In addition casual labour will be required to collect, transport and stack gravel and sand for concrete. This can be done at any time in advance of construction; in an agricultural community there is usually a slack period between harvest and the sowing season when volunteer village workers can most easily contribute their efforts. As a rough guide to the quantities that will be needed take the estimated depth of the well (in metres), halving this figure will give the number of cubic metres of gravel that will be required, halving it again will give the sand requirements. (These figures include an allowance for building the wellhead. They may have to be increased if difficult soil conditions call for extra lining thickness.)

A nightwatchman to keep animals and children away from the excavation and to protect tools and equipment from pilfering is sometimes considered a necessity.

CHAPTER 4   PREPARATORY WORK

Community awareness and needs

An improved water source, especially one that is to be constructed by self-help methods, must be genuinely wanted by those whom it is designed to serve. This statement is not as trivial as might at first appear.

Every community, every individual, already has a source of drinking water of some sort, otherwise life would be impossible. It may be inadequate, inconvenient, unreliable, dangerous to the consumer (or all of these), but it exists. If a new well is to be constructed, if the villagers are expected to do the work and to maintain it in good order afterwards, if they are going to be asked to contribute toward the cement and steel, they must be convinced before construction starts that it will be to their advantage. In other words, they must want it.

In some cases the advantages will be obvious. If the existing source dries up periodically, if it is at a distance involving long hours of water carrying, if there is congestion at peak periods of water collection, a more ample and more convenient supply will be welcomed. Elsewhere the benefits may not be so apparent. If the present source is a nearby river or pond, even though this may be polluted or infested with parasites, a new well may merely represent additional labour in drawing water from a considerable depth, unless the health implications of the proposals are fully understood by all consumers. Without this understanding drinking water may still be drawn from the old, unsafe source even if the new well is satisfactory in every way.

The first step in planning a new water supply is therefore to investigate the existing source, to determine its inadequacies, to produce the arguments in favour of improvement and to convince everyone concerned of their validity.

Local political and religious leaders, teachers and others influential in the village will be of assistance here; the planner's task will be easiest when the people themselves are so convinced that they demand action.

The next step will often be to fit the proposed improved supply, in this case a hand dug well, into a larger programme. This may be of two kinds — a series of wells to be constructed in a number of neighbouring villages (which will materially reduce the cost and difficulty of sinking each well), or a number of improvements to the hygiene of one community (in which case the well might be combined with latrine construction, surface drainage, slaughter slabs, market improvements or other measures designed to raise health standards). Discussions with local people and the fixing of priorities by them will add to the goodwill here.

As regards the water supply improvement the next stage is to determine whether well digging is the most suitable method of supply. Comparison of wells with other sources, such as rainwater catchments, protected springs, treated surface water supplies and the like is outside the scope of this manual. It is assumed that the safety, quality and reliability of ground water has already led to the decision that a well should be used or, alternatively, that no other suitable source exists.

The next question is the number of wells that will be required to meet the needs of the community. Experience has shown that with a good aquifer a single well can, at a pinch, supply the domestic water requirements of about five hundred persons (say 120-150 families), though half that number is considered more suitable if congestion at peak periods is to be avoided. If domestic animals are to be watered, the number of families that can be served from each well will be correspondingly reduced. Allowance must also be made for special demands, e.g. a market that brings in people from outside; a clinic or school that does not have its own well; the use of well water for village industries (such as dyepits or blacksmith's workshops) or for growing vegetables during the dry season. In all but the very smallest communities it is better to have separate specially protected wells for domestic supplies, with extra wells for these other uses.

Before starting construction it will also be necessary to decide upon the method of extraction intended to be used since this will determine the design of the wellhead. A pump on a sealed well top is hygienically preferable, but this will involve not only its capital cost but also its future maintenance. While stressing its desirability it is assumed (for the purposes of this manual) that open wells are the best that can be managed as an initial step in most isolated rural areas.

To sum up: observation and discussion on the lines indicated above have led to the decision that the existing water source needs improvement and that well sinking is the way in which that improvement can best be undertaken. The number of wells needed by the community has been decided upon and the villagers have agreed to participate in their construction on a self-help basis.

Locating the well

Obviously it is of no use to embark on a well sinking project or programme unless there are at least reasonable prospects of obtaining ground water in adequate quantities. It is also important that the conditions of the subsoil are such that the methods intended to be used will be capable of penetrating to the aquifer.

In areas where the aquifer and subsoil conditions are completely unknown, professional advice should be called in. Although the actual financial loss incurred by digging and abandoning an abortive well may well not be very large, the disappointment and wasted effort may sour the villagers and prejudice them against other self-help works in the future. Advice from an experienced geologist, possibly assisted by geophysical equipment, can not only help to avoid such a failure but can also be of great assistance in forecasting the depth and quantity of water to be expected and in warning of special difficulties that may be encountered. In most countries there exist government geological survey departments having knowledge of local conditions and their specialised advice is always worth seeking and following wherever any doubt exists.

Having said this, there are many areas where there are sufficient indications as to the presence of groundwater. Of these the most obvious is the existence of other wells in the vicinity. Although geological conditions can (and often do) change materially over short distances there are, nevertheless, large tracts over which any changes are small and gradual, so that conditions in one well may be repeated in another some distance away. The advice of 'traditional' well sinkers (whose knowledge of the country may be excellent even if their construction techniques are old fashioned and unhygienic) should not be despised. If the sinkers themselves are unavailable or uncooperative a reconnaissance of old wells or other excavations (e.g. borrow pits or brick workings) in the neighbourhood will often yield valuable information.

It should be remembered that subsoil changes are often (though by no means always) accompanied by surface indications, and it should be assumed, in the absence of contrary evidence, that rocky outcrops, cliffs or upthrusts will break the continuity of an aquifer. Again, if there is any doubt, a geologist should be consulted.

Another favourable indication of an aquifer is the presence of springs. When one or more of these issue on a hillside or at its base a well sunk further up the slope will usually tap the saturated strata that feed the spring water, and because the water has not yet emerged from the ground its quality is likely to be better.

Similarly wells sunk in the flood plain of a river, or close to a stream, lake or swamp, may produce ample water free from the contamination that makes the open surface water unsafe. A warning should be given here — often such areas are of impermeable material such as clay which, though saturated, will not permit water to flow into the well. Since aquifers of this type are usually at a shallow depth from the surface it often pays to dig a trial pit (unlined) down to the expected depth and by pumping or the use of buckets to see how quickly it can be emptied.

The location of the well may therefore have to be outside the village, considerations such as geological advice, local information or topographical inspection being taken into account. In other cases it may be apparent that the precise spot will have little bearing on its yield; this will particularly apply where a number of old or insanitary wells bear witness to the existence of a widely dispersed water table. In these circumstances location will depend on other considerations, e.g. the point at which it will be closest to the majority of the population, proximity to the market place, distance from latrines, rubbish tips or other potential sources of pollution, ease of access by villagers, good drainage of the surrounding area, adequate working space for the construction team and those who will draw water from the completed well, and so on. Political considerations cannot always be ignored; there will sometimes be pressure to sink the well close to the house of the village headman or other influential citizen whose support for the project is desired, and compromise may be called for.

Rough estimate of labour and materials for reinforced concrete lined wells

Before starting work it will be necessary to collect materials; cement and reinforcing steel will have to be bought or otherwise obtained, gravel and sand will have to be brought to the site and stacked ready for use. If a pump is to be fitted it is usually desirable (though not always essential) to have this on hand ready for installation on completion of the well. Some idea of the quantities required is essential, otherwise either too much material may be obtained or, alternatively, work may be held up through lack of supplies. The length of time over which labour will be employed is another item that will need to be forecast.

The most important variable in wells sunk to the dimensions and by the techniques described is the finished depth; less important factors include lining thickness (which may have to be increased in bad ground, or may sometimes be omitted in part when sinking through such materials as sandstone), the design of the intake and wellhead, slowing down of work in ground containing boulders. It is usually convenient to make the first, rough, estimate in terms of well depth, making a suitable allowance one way or the other for the other factors described.

When several wells are to be sunk over-estimating on the first one will not matter much since surplus material can be used for subsequent construction. It will be easier to forecast the depth of the others on the experience of the first. If a single well is to be sunk the only basis of estimating will be the evidence of water table level in other excavations or spring levels. The well depth may be assumed to be the distance from ground surface to three metres below the water table at the driest time of the year.

The following 'rule of thumb' figures may be useful for estimating and ordering materials, assuming the ground is good and the wellhead simple.

Cement   120kg per metre depth, plus 200kg for wellhead and apron.

Reinforcing rods   30 metres of 8mm diameter rod per metre depth, plus 50 metres of 15mm diameter (single item only) for the caisson intake (3m deep).

Gravel   ½ cubic metre per metre depth.

Sand   ¼ cubic metre per metre depth.

Construction labour (team of 6 men plus headman) 2 working days per metre depth, plus 10 working days for preparation, wellhead and clearing site.

Where the nature of the ground is not known, and when the well team is inexperienced, it may be wise to increase all these figures by, say, 25%.

It is worth while to keep a close record of time and material costs during the sinking of the first well so that more accurate estimates can be made for subsequent ones. This is especially important if the first well is to be subject to closer supervision than will be possible later; a check on quantities will show how efficiently the less supervised construction is being carried out.

Equipment

Chapter 18 gives a schedule of the tools and equipment normally considered the minimum necessary for a team undertaking a programme of well construction, followed by some notes on the use of the various items and some suggested alternatives to reduce costs where only a single well (or very few) are to be sunk. It should be stressed that the schedule has been compiled on the basis of actual experience in Africa and elsewhere; wells undoubtedly can be sunk with substitute equipment and fewer tools, but sinking is almost certain to take longer and cost more. When one or two wells only are contemplated this additional cost may be less than the amount saved on the purchase of the tools, but with a programme covering a number of wells the right equipment is always a good investment. Above all, even with a single well, safety of the sinkers must not be prejudiced by the omission of head protection or by the use of inferior quality ropes.

Portability is an important factor when equipment has to be carried from one site to another, especially where road access is difficult. The heavier items, such as the headframe, steel lining shutters and moulds, should always be capable of being dismantled so that each part can be carried by one man — all the items described in the schedule fulfill this condition.

Records

It is most desirable that a record should be made on the completion of any well. Not only will this be useful if deepening or reconditioning is needed at some future time, but the information may be of assistance to anyone wishing to dig another well nearby.

A well record should describe the strata through which the shaft has been sunk, the level and thickness of the aquifer(s) tapped and any special difficulties encountered during sinking, e.g. boulders, sugar sand, swelling shale or hard rock. The length of the shaft lining and of telescoped caisson should be noted, remembering that the length of 'overlap' cannot be observed once the well is finished. The intake should be described, whether the water enters through the side or bottom, whether side openings are through porous concrete or through weepholes, the top and bottom levels of the permeable section of the shaft and (in the case of bottom intakes) the thickness and grading of any gravel filter. None of these details can be easily verified when the well is full of water.

The precise point from which depths have been measured should be clearly stated, whether this is ground level or the top of the headwall, so that any silting can be checked easily by dropping a measuring tape from the surface, and the water level fluctuation in the well at different seasons can be similarly observed.

When the well is sealed and fitted with a pump the record is even more important, since observation will be more difficult. In such cases a description of the pump, rods, suction and rising main should be added, the depths at which the pump strainer and barrel have been set, and any information (such as diameter and type of pump leather, type of foot valve) added to enable spares to be obtained without first removing the pump from the well.

In extensive well sinking programmes it is common practice to keep this information in a central register, identifying each well with a number which is clearly marked in the wet concrete of the well head during completion. Sometimes the depth of the well is similarly marked to assist anyone making maintenance checks.

PART II   STANDARD WELL
SINKING PRACTICE

CHAPTER 5   SUMMARY OF METHODS

The following eight chapters are intended to be complete in themselves, comprising a detailed set of instructions on the various stages of digging and lining a well with reinforced concrete. They are addressed primarily to those who will be responsible for actually carrying out the work in the field.

For the sake of simplicity and clarity they deal with one particular type of well only — a reinforced concrete lined circular shaft well of 1.3 metres internal diameter, excavated through sedimentary soils to an open aquifer having a water table some 20-30 metres below ground surface. The wellhead is open, extraction of water will be by buckets and ropes, and construction is by 'self-help' methods employing local labour.

Conditions and resources will obviously vary from place to place and will call for the use of different materials and techniques in certain cases. A number of alternatives have been described, but these have been set out in Part III so that the continuity of this part of the manual is not interrupted. Descriptions of the equipment required and other general information will be found in Part IV for the same reason.

The technique of well sinking described is a combination of two methods; the first is known as 'sink-and-line' or 'dig-down-build-up', and is used for the shaft from ground level down to the water table. The second is called 'caissoning', and this method is employed for constructing the intake and that part of the shaft that lies within the aquifer.

In the 'dig-down-build-up' method the shaft is excavated to a greater diameter than the finished dimension, after which a lining is built up from the bottom by pouring concrete behind removable shutters. The advantages of this method is that a close, strong, waterproof and permanent bond is made with the walls of the excavation, excluding contaminated water that may be in the soil near the surface, and giving a smooth, regular internal finish to the shaft. Since, for reasons of safety, it is generally unwise to leave too great a length of shaft wall unsupported, any well of depth greater than about 5 metres is sunk and lined in a series of stages or 'lifts', each being completed before the next lift is started.

As soon as the water table is reached the method is changed to 'caissoning', by which a tube is built upwards from the bottom of the well and allowed to sink under its own weight to its final position as the soil is excavated from within it. The outside diameter of the caisson is slightly less than the 1.3 metres internal diameter of the lining while its inside measurement must be sufficient to enable a man to work inside to carry out the excavation.

The sequence illustrated below is of a shallow single-lift well, and also shows the final stage of construction — completion of the wellhead:—

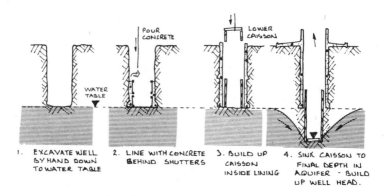

Construction of shallow hand dug well.

CHAPTER 6 PREPARATION OF SITE AND SETTING UP OF HEADFRAME – CONSTRUCTION STAGE 1

Preparing the site

The first step is to clear the chosen site of vegetation to provide a working space of about 15 metres radius around the well. Roughly level the ground, and locate the centre of the well on a high spot to prevent surface run-off from rain storms washing into the well. Mark out areas for the collected sand and gravel, and construct a shelter to store the cement, tools and the concrete bricks that you will make. The nature of this shelter will vary according to the season, location, local materials available, whether there is danger from thieves, fire or animals, but may merely consist of a grass walled hut with a thatched roof. It is usual to appoint a watchman to guard the store overnight.

Setting out the working area is more important than at first appears, the objective being to ensure that there is adequate working space for each operation, that no stage of the work hampers another and that the distance over which heavy loads have to be moved is kept to the minimum. Care at this stage can improve construction efficiency later.

It is, for example, essential that the sand and gravel for concreting is kept clean, so the excavated material from the well must be removed and dumped clear of the stock piles of aggregate. These in turn must be sited close enough to the mixing slab to reduce double handling, while the mixing slab itself should be placed about 2 metres from the headframe (on the opposite side from the winch) so that a single movement can transfer a full bucket of concrete from slab to well mouth. The offset pegs used to plumb the well should be so fixed that they will not be knocked by kibbles or by caisson rings when these are being lowered into the well. A typical layout is shown overleaf but this will be subject to variation

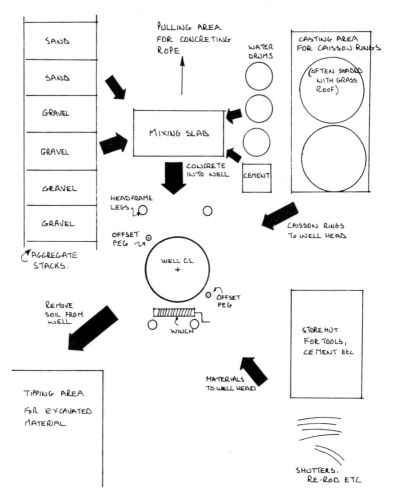

SAND

SAND

GRAVEL

GRAVEL

GRAVEL

GRAVEL

AGGREGATE
STACKS.

PULLING AREA
FOR CONCRETING
ROPE

WATER
DRUMS

MIXING SLAB

CASTING AREA
FOR CAISSON RING'S

(OFTEN SHADED
WITH GRASS
ROOF)

CONCRETE
INTO WELL

CEMENT

HEADFRAME
LEGS

OFFSET
PEG

WELL CL.
+

OFFSET
PEG

CAISSON RINGS
TO WELL HEAD

REMOVE
SOIL FROM
WELL

WINCH

STORE HUT
FOR TOOLS,
CEMENT ETC

TIPPING AREA

FOR EXCAVATED
MATERIAL

MATERIALS
TO WELL HEAD

SHUTTERS.
RE-ROD ETC

Well site laid out for easy handling of materials and equipment.

according to local site conditions, direction of access, position of disposal area of excavated material and similar factors.

Sand and gravel will have to be brought to the site; preferably it should all have been collected in readiness before work starts, but some at least must already be at the site. To ensure that the amounts are adequate and that work will not be held up for want of concreting materials it is usual to stack the aggregate in easily measured flat topped heaps,

56

rectangular in plan, one metre high. Corner pegs projecting one metre out of the ground are driven as guides, the space between them is cleared of grass and roughly levelled. If aggregate is going to continue to arrive during construction it will be easier to check quantities if several measured piles are made and used one after another. Thus if the well is expected to be about 24 metres deep 12 cubic metres of gravel and 6 cubic metres of sand will be required, which could be conveniently stacked in three heaps of 2 metres x 2 metres (for gravel) and two of 2 metres x 1.5 metres (for sand), each heap being 1 metre high.

Water will probably be brought to the site in drums (which must be thoroughly cleaned of all traces of oil or other contaminants) and these will be placed reasonably close to the mixing slab. Again, to avoid holding up work, plenty of spare capacity should be provided.

Cement will be taken in bags from the store hut as required, and the nearer to the mixing slab this is sited, the less labour will be used in carrying.

Assembling the headframe

The first operation is to erect the headframe centrally over the chosen site of the well shaft. The type of frame described in Chapter 18 was developed after considerable experiment in Nigeria and is strong, portable and efficient. Cheaper substitutes can be used for isolated wells (some are described later in this manual), but it is strongly recommended that wherever possible, a properly fabricated headframe should be chosen. In terms of speed, safety and efficiency it will prove a sound investment especially when a large well construction programme is planned.

The frame shown is made of angle iron sections bolted together. It is fitted with a winch and brake and a device that enables the hoisting drum to be disconnected from the handles but not from the brake; this prevents accidents with the handle during lowering operations. Flexible wire rope with a fibre core passes from the hoisting drum over the main 'headsheave' pulley and the geared winch is capable of raising or lowering the heaviest loads that will be encountered — men, full kibbles or concrete caisson rings. An auxiliary pulley is provided for concreting operations; its use will be described later. The total height of the headframe is a little over 4 metres.

The headframe is set upright over the position chosen for the wellshaft. The four 'feet' of the headframe must be on solid ground, otherwise a slab of stone or small quantity of concrete must be placed under each. It is important that once the centre point of the well has been fixed, the frame should not move out of position.

Casting the mixing slab

A slab for mixing concrete is now constructed about 2 metres from the headframe on the opposite side to that carrying the winch. The slab may be made by levelling off an area about 2 metres square, removing grass and vegetation, covering this area with gravel tamped to a finished thickness of 5 cms and spreading cement mortar (4 parts sand to 1 part cement) over the surface with a trowel to make a smooth finish. It is an advantage to form a lip in this mortar around the edge to prevent the loss of cement slurry if concrete is mixed care-lessly. The slab should be covered with wet sacking or cement bags for two or three days to allow it to set hard before use:—

Casting the mixing slab.

Centering the well

Before you begin to dig the well, you will need to fix the point on the ground through which the vertical central axis of the well will pass. This point is known as the centre point, (C.P.) and is used throughout the construction of the well.

To do this a plumb bob (or string with a suitable weight attached) is lowered from the headsheave pulley on the side opposite the winch, i.e. from the point at which the main hoisting rope will descend. Mark the point where the plumb bob strikes the ground by driving a short length of steel reinforcing rod (re-rod) into the ground, then draw out a circle of 1 metre radius using a stick and measured length of rope. The CP of the well will of course be lost as soon as you begin to dig and it is necessary to transfer it to permanent offset pegs outside the excavation. During construction, the CP is transferred from these offset pegs down into the well by the use of a plumb line and the top plumbing rod; in this way, you will be able to keep your well truly vertical. To transfer the CP, the top plumbing rod is fitted over the offset pegs, and the plumb line suspended from the mid point. This procedure will be described in detail later.

On opposite sides of the circle you have drawn out, excavate two small holes about 25cm deep, and 25cm square in such a position that the pegs will be protected by the legs of the headframe from chance knocks or damage, then cast the two offset pegs in these holes. The offset pegs are made from lengths of 8mm re-rod and the concrete is carried up 15cm above the ground. Old tins with the top and bottom removed may be used as shuttering for the concrete surrounding these pegs. Place the top plumbing rod over the offset pegs and adjust these in the wet concrete until they are vertical and of uniform height, making sure that the rod lifts off easily:—

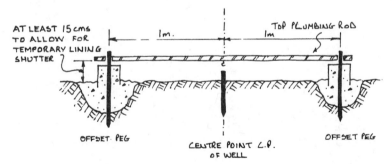

Installing offset pegs.

Give the concrete several days to cure and set hard before you use the pegs.

CHAPTER 7   EXCAVATING AND LINING TOP SECTION
— CONSTRUCTION STAGE 2

Constructing temporary lining at well mouth

Most of the accidents that occur in well construction are
caused by the collapse of the loose surface soil layers into the
well or by tools and materials being accidentally knocked
into the well.

You can reduce these risks by lining temporarily the top
metre or so of excavation before you dig any deeper. One of
the 1 metre deep concrete shutters makes a useful temporary
support; it is fixed into place and the well excavated and
lined inside its protection. It is removed when the R.C. lining
is poured up to the level of its base, the sides are then cut
back and the lining taken on up to the surface. The top section or lift of the lining will then be continuous and waterproof, which prevents contaminated water from soaking in
down the sides of the well through construction joints.

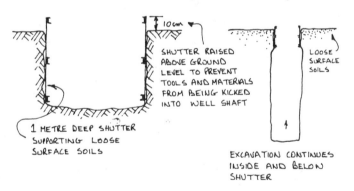

Temporary lining at well top.

First a circle of 65cm radius is marked around the CP and
a hole 90cm deep dug to this size and shape. A set of 1 metre
high shutters is assembled on the surface and lowered into

the excavation with 10cm of its length projecting above ground level.

It is important that this temporary lining should be accurately centred and its sides vertical, otherwise buckets and kibbles lowered later may foul it and spill their loads. Fit the top plumbing rod over the offset pegs and check the lining position, also check the verticality of the sides with a plumb bob, adjusting if necessary by packing and ramming soil outside the lining shutter.

Excavating the first lift of the well

When the temporary lining has been set in position it will be safe to dig down to a depth of 5 metres below the ground surface. This will give a depth below the bottom of the temporary shutter of 4.1 metres.

The tools used for sinking are miners' picks and bars for loosening the soil, short handled shovels for filling the loosened materials into the kibble (hoisting bucket) and mattocks for accurately trimming the shaft wall. All these tools, together with some notes on their respective uses are described and listed in Chapters 18 and 19.

Excavation is normally carried out in layers of about 10cm at a time, keeping the exposed surface at the bottom reasonably level — this makes for easier working. Until the sinkers become experienced it will be found advantageous to excavate rather less than the full diameter until at least 1 metre has been sunk, and then trim back accurately to the correct dimensions. This is one of the trickiest operations in well digging; the degree of accuracy of the trimming will affect the lining thickness and consequently the cost of the well. It is worth remembering that one centimetre additional thickness means 15% more concrete in the lining. It is therefore important to instruct the sinkers to carry out the trimming procedure with the utmost care.

Part of the equipment listed consists of two sets of trimming rods, the 'short' set having a total length of a fraction less than 1.30m, the 'long' set just less than 1.45m. Although they can be made of timber they are much easier to use if each set consists of two lengths of re-rod (15mm is a convenient thickness) riveted together exactly in the centre suficiently loosely to enable them to be opened out into a cross during use, or folded together for storage at other times.

A hook or eyelet must be attached to the rivet to enable them to hang level from a plumb line, the upper end of which is fastened to the centre of the top plumbing rod.

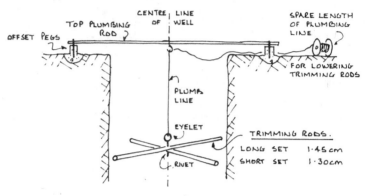

Trimming rods.

It helps to avoid possible mistakes if a dab of different coloured paint is applied so that there can be no confusion between long and short sets of rods.

Fit the short set first and roughly trim the shaft so that they may pass up and down, and turn on the plumbing line, without touching the shaft wall. Then, starting at one level, cut four notches into the soil of the wall 7.5cm deep and fit the long set so that their ends hang freely in these notches. Working round the circle with a trimming mattock cut a band a few centimetres high within which the long trimming rods will revolve freely. Work up and down from this band

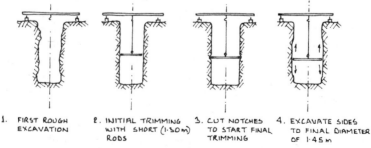

Stages in excavating and trimming.

until the whole of the shaft wall is trimmed to a vertical cylinder of 145cm diameter. When the concrete lining of 7.5cm thickness has been installed (as will be described) the finished internal diameter of the well will be 1.30 metres.

An alternative method of accurately excavating the sides of the shaft is shown below. In this technique, a piece of re-rod is driven into the base of the well under a plumb bob at every 10cm layer of cut. The sides of the well are then cut back to a radius of 72.5cm around this centre-rod, and are checked using a measuring rod:—

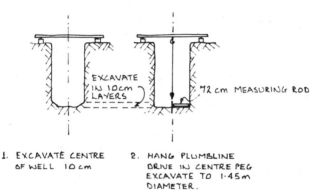

1. EXCAVATE CENTRE
   OF WELL 10 cm

2. HANG PLUMBLINE
   DRIVE IN CENTRE PEG
   EXCAVATE TO 1·45m
   DIAMETER.

Excavate and trim in layers.

The excavated material is brought to the surface in a kibble attached to a rope which passes over the main head-sheave of the headframe to the geared hoist of the winch. At all times during raising and lowering the kibble there should be two men on the winch handles and the headman should have control of the brake.

The kibble or bucket that is used to lift out excavated material or water during the sinking work must be strong and water tight, with a loop in the handle. It is often made wider at the centre than between the lips, to reduce the risks of fouling and tipping as it is pulled up. The handle should be attached to the top rim of the kibble; a handle attached to the middle of the kibble will cause the bucket to tilt if the safety handle is accidently lifted.

A simple safety catch is welded across one side of the bucket mouth, which fastens onto the handle during use to prevent accidental tipping. The kibble is not replaced by an empty kibble after it has been hoisted up full of materials — it is pulled away from the well mouth, the safety catch unfastened, and the contents emptied. The kibbles are made with steel strips welded around the rims and base to withstand wear and tear. They are attached to the lifting ropes by a safety tumbler hook, which makes connection and disconnection quick and positive while preventing accidental release. These and other equipment items are described and illustrated in Chapter 18.

It is of course possible to construct wells using ordinary buckets or baskets in place of the specially made kibbles, but experienced well diggers do not recommend them. The extra investment in a good, sound kibble is amply repaid in speed, safety, and durability. You must remember that a kibble full of water or soil may have a weight in excess of 75 kgm. The men digging in the well will have greater confidence if they are sure that the kibble or its contents will not accidently fall down the well on top of them

The procedure described above is continued and the first lift excavated to a depth of 5.0 metres unless the side of the well begins to collapse, or unless water is struck before that depth. Only if the soil is particularly strong and firm can you risk continuing excavation any deeper before lining with concrete.

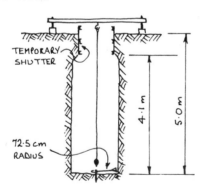

TEMPORARY SHUTTER

4.1 m

5.0 m

72.5 cm RADIUS

Excavate to 5m below ground level -- with a radius of 72.5cm

Lining the top lift of the well

a) Setting the 0.5 metre deep shutters

A set of 130cm diameter shutters, 0.5 metre deep, is oiled on the surface, and lowered down the well for assembly. The first set of shutters will be placed accurately to carry the lining shutters on top, and to support the re-rods.

The assembled shutters are blocked up level, using a spirit level and centred using the 65cm radius plumbing rods:—

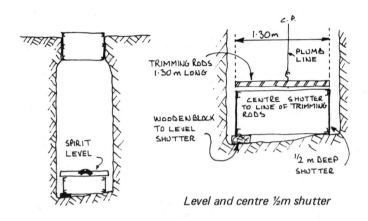

Level and centre ½m shutter

The short trimming rods are suspended on the end of the plumb line from the top plumbing rod, and are allowed to hang just above the top of the blocked up shutters. The shutters are adjusted until the outside edge lies directly below the ends of the rods; the shutter will now be truly central in the well. It is of the greatest importance that this first set of shutters is accurately positioned, as it will determine the position of the shutters set above. If it is out of position or tilted, the whole of the top lift will be thrown out of line, and this will be very difficult to correct.

b) *Fixing the reinforcing rods*

The next step is to assemble the re-rod cage around the side of the well. The 8mm diameter vertical re-rods will be inserted behind the bottom shutter, which will then be back filled with soil to hold both the re-rods and the shutter steady.

The number of vertical re-rods you must use will vary according to the nature of the ground. Occasionally, no re-rods are necessary although this only happens when you are sinking through sandstone or similar self supporting ground; the purpose of the lining is then not to support the ground but to keep out contaminated surface water. In bad collap-

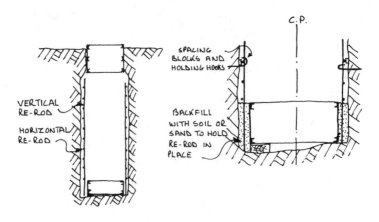

Fixing the reinforcing rods.

sing ground you may need to use as many as 30 vertical re-rods with walls of up to 15cm thickness. It is difficult to state exactly how many rods are needed in any particular case, but the table given below is often quoted by well diggers:—

Soil condition	Fissured rock or sandstone	Consolidated soils	Loose sand Swelling shales
Vertical re-rod (Number) 8mm diameter	None	15	30
Horizontal re-rod (Number for each metre depth) 8mm diameter	None	3	4

The vertical re-rods are cut to a length of about 4 metres and fixed behind the first shutter, uniformly around the walls of the well.

The rings of horizontal re-rod are made up on the surface by bending the re-rod around pegs knocked into the ground to form a circle.

The radius of the circle to the outside of the pegs is 69cms.

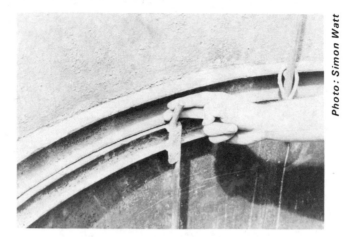

Photo 10   Steel Shutters from Rolled Channel and Thin Steel Plate, For Casting In-Situ Concrete Lining — Placing lug to hold shutter above in place. — Upper Volta.

Photo 11   b) Reinforced concrete cast in-situ behind metal shutters. — Upper Volta.

Photo: Simon Watt

Photo 12   Steel Shutters from Rolled Channel and Thin
Steel Plate, For Casting In-Situ Concrete Lining —
c) Welded steel shutters, 0.5 metre deep. These will have a
working life of at least 10 years if they are looked after.
Cost about $300/metre (1975 costs).

Photo: Simon Watt

Photo 13   d) Shutter wedge, these are unbolted and
pulled out to release shutters from well.

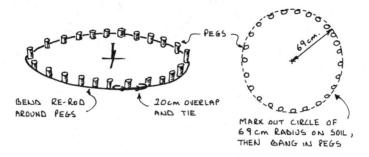

PEGS

BEND RE-ROD AROUND PEGS

20cm OVERLAP AND TIE

69cm

MARK OUT CIRCLE OF 69cm RADIUS ON SOIL, THEN BANG IN PEGS

Making up the horizontal re-rod rings.

The rods are given an overlap of 20cms and the ends bound securely together with soft iron binding wire. The rings are then lowered down the shaft and fitted around the outside of the vertical re-rods, where they are bound into place using soft iron binding wire at the spacings recommended above. They will have an external clearance of about 3cms with the sides of the excavated well. Pieces of stone or concrete 3cms thick are packed behind the horizontal re-rods, and the rings are adjusted to be truly circular.

With the horizontal circles tied securely to the vertical re-rods, the reinforcement cage will be strong and securely held together. The external concrete cover over the horizontal re-rods will therefore be 3cms and the internal cover of the vertical re-rods to the inside of the well will also be 3cms. Short hooks of bent re-rod are driven into the sides of the well around the vertical re-rods, to prevent the cage from moving whilst the concrete lining is being poured.

c) Setting the shutters, mixing and pouring the concrete

You can now line the well with concrete poured behind additional shutters, which are assembled and positioned on top of the first shutter.

A second set of shutters, 1 metre deep, is oiled on the surface, lowered down the well, assembled and fixed in place on the first shutters. The shutter plumbing rod is used to check the correct position, and a spirit level is used to make sure that the shutter is sitting level; then wooden blocks are used, if needed, to level up the shutter.

The concrete is mixed by hand on the mixing slab to the proportions of 1:2½:5 (cement:sand:gravel). It is difficult to judge these proportions with accuracy using a shovel, and bottomless gauging boxes should be used. Make up as part of your well sinking gear two boxes 75cm x75cm in plan, one of 30cm depth for gravel, the other of 15cm depth for sand. When mixed with 50kgm of cement, these quantities give the correct proportions, and in quantity enough to fill 0.5 metre depth of pour at 7.5 cm thickness.

Make sure that the water you use to make the concrete is clean and free from organic matter, oil or suspended clay. Impurities will ruin your concrete.

To mix the concrete, spread the gauged gravel on the mixing slab, the gauged sand evenly over the gravel, and cover the sand with correct amount of cement. Then shovel the whole into a pile on one side of the slab. With a man on either side of the pile, facing each other and working their shovels together, turn the whole heap over once to form a pile at the other end of the slab, and then turn it back again to its former position. Thus the whole mass has been turned twice 'dry'.

Flatten the pile, make a hollow in the top, and add water a little at a time (a watering can with a perforated rose makes the job easier but is not essential) and turn the heap over twice as before, this time 'wet'. It is not possible here to say how much water will be required, since this will depend upon how moist the sand and gravel were before mixing, but a rough guide is to take a handful of the final mixture and squeeze it as hard as possible. If the consistency is right it will just be possible (but only just) to squeeze a few drops of liquid out of the handful.

Too much water will make the concrete weak and liable to leak out between the joints of the shutters. Too little will make it unworkable. It is always easier to add more water than to correct excessive moisture by adding extra aggregate and cement.

Never make up more concrete than can be used within two hours. If work is held up for longer than this the concrete should not be used in the well; never try to add more water and remix old concrete. To stop the mixture drying out on the slab under a hot sun while it is being bucketed into the well cover with plastic sheeting, wet hessian or old cement bags.

Photo 14   Mixing the Concrete by Hand on the Mixing Tray — Low walls prevent accidental loss of cement slurry. In the photograph a hoe is being used; square shovels make the work easier. — Upper Volta.

Photo 15   Lowering the Concrete into the Well in the Special Bucket — Upper Volta.

Good concrete can only be produced by the proper mixing of the right materials. It is important to make sure that the above procedure is carried out in detail every time.

Measuring and mixing the concrete.

The concrete is now lowered down the well in the concreting bucket, and you must take care that it does not catch on any projection and spill its contents on the well sinkers below. The winch is not used for lowering the concrete bucket, which is carried by a 6mm rope over the auxiliary headsheave. This is partly because this method of raising and lowering comparatively small loads is considerably quicker than winching, and partly because for all shutters above the bottom two the well sinker will need to be supported in a bosun's chair on the main rope to pour the lining concrete.

A short, strong piece of wood is tied securely to the upper end of the lifting rope; the man doing the lowering walks with the handle away from the well until the rope is tight, — a second man lifts the concrete bucket and guides it out over the well, and the first man walks back to the well, holding the rope and controlling the rate of descent. Lifting the bucket is the reverse process. This method of lowering and raising the concrete bucket reduces the risk of jerky movements which could spill the contents.

The concrete is poured carefully between the shutter and the walls, evenly all around to prevent weight building up on one side and shifting the shutter, and the concrete is tamped using a piece of re-rod to remove air pockets. Fill the space up until the concrete reaches a few centimentres from

72

the top; this will give a sound joint between this pour and the next one on top. The top of the concrete should be left rough so that a good bond is made with the next pour above. Whenever a break in the work occurs, either overnight or during a meal break, the surface of the concrete must be scraped clean and well wetted before the new mix is poured on. If soil falls onto the wet concrete, remove all the soil and scrape out the layer of wet concrete in contact with the soil.

When the second shutter has been filled with concrete (the first shutter is filled with earth), the first curb is made. A curb is made for each 5 metre lift of the lining to provide support against the downward movement of the lining during digging. It is made by cutting a triangular sectioned groove in the side of the excavation immediately above the top of the second shutter. This groove is 20cm deep all round, and 20cm high at the well face, — check the shape using the curb gauge. Re-rod pins are driven into the groove, the hooked ends holding each vertical re-rod, and are also attached to one of the horizontal rings. Take care when excavating this groove that you do not spill soil onto the concrete below; if this occurs, scrape the loose soil carefully away from the wet concrete. Better still, cover the top of the concrete with a sheet of plastic, cement bag etc., for protection.

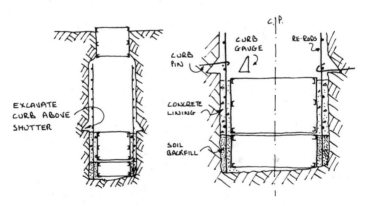

Cutting out the curb for the lining lift.

Concrete is now hand filled into the curb all round, and a third set of shutters 1m high is lowered, levelled, checked for centre and bolted into place, the space behind being then filled with concrete. With the fixing of the third shutter, the top will be too high for a man to work from the bottom of the well, and pouring and tamping must be done from the bosun's chair suspended from the surface, or from a scaffolding plank fitted temporarily on the ribs of one of the shutters. The latter method is probably safer but slower as the plank must be moved each time a new shutter is fitted.

A fourth set of shutters is oiled, lowered, assembled, placed and back filled with concrete in exactly the same way, and at this stage the top of the fourth shutter will be about 60cm below the level of the temporary lining supporting the surface soil.

d) Finishing the first lift to the well

The temporary lining shutter is now removed, and the sides of the well cut back to allow the concrete lining to be poured up to the surface.

The shutter is attached to the lifting rope, it is unbolted, taken apart, and removed from the well. The sides of the well are dug out to a diameter of 160cm, extending from the surface down to the top of the fourth shutter. The concrete in the fourth shutter is covered with sacking or other material, to protect it from falling soil.

The tops of the vertical re-rod in the lift already placed, are bent over into a hook of 5cm diameter and extra lengths of hooked re-rod are securely attached to these with an over-

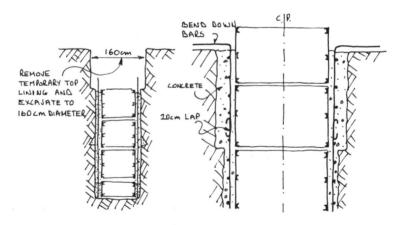

Finishing the first lift.

74

lap of at least 20cm using soft iron wire. Extra horizontal re-rod circles are also fixed and bound to form a cage.

Shutters are again oiled, lowered and placed on top of the fourth shutter. The space behind them is carefully filled to the surface with concrete, and the bars bent down onto the ground.

The extra thickness of concrete lining in the top 1.5 metres of the first lift will provide a solid base for the wellhead structure which will be described in Chapter 10.

At this stage the vertical re-rods which have been bent down at the top of the well are covered with a very weak mortar layer 10cm thick, made from a mix not stronger than 1:15 (cement:sand). This weak layer can be broken away at the completion of the well and the re-rods bent up to make the well head:—

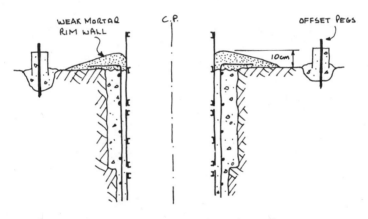

Building up the temporary rim wall.

The weak mortar layer will form a temporary rim around the wellhead, keeping the bent re-rod out of the way and also preventing tools from being kicked into the well.

The first lift is now completed and consists of 4.5 metres of reinforced concrete lining supported by shuttering, 10cm of weak mortar walling above ground level and an extra half metre of unlined excavation at the bottom of the well.

The shutters should be left in place for as long as possible before they are removed. They will protect the 'green' concrete from accidental knocks before it has properly cured, they will prevent moisture loss from the concrete and they will help to support the well until the concrete is strong enough. It is of great advantage to have extra sets of shutters which can be used to build the second lift without waiting for the first lift to cure. In any case the shutters should not be stripped from the first lift within seven days of the concrete being poured.

CHAPTER 8   SINKING AND LINING SHAFT TO
AQUIFER — CONSTRUCTION STAGE 3

Constructing the second lift

The second lift is now excavated whilst the shutters to the
first lift are left in position. Remove the earth-filled shutter
and clean the re-rods with a wire brush.

Excavate the second lift to a depth of 4.65 metres below
the concrete lining of the first lift in exactly the same way as
already described. The lower ends of the re-rods of the first
lift will be projecting 0.5 metre below the concrete — each of
these should be bent into a hook of 5cm diameter.

The procedure for the construction of the lining and curb
of the second lift is exactly the same as that for the first
lift, except that there will be a gap of 15 cm between the
concrete lining of the second and first lifts. This gap is needed
to pour concrete behind the shutters of this second and subsequent lifts and a funnel or chute from beaten scrap metal
will be needed to prevent the waste of spilled concrete. The
top of the re-rods of the second lift should be bent into a
5cm diameter hook and tied with soft iron wire to the re-rods
hanging down from the first lift, with an overlap of at least
20cm. The hooks allow the re-rod to grip into the concrete
lining.

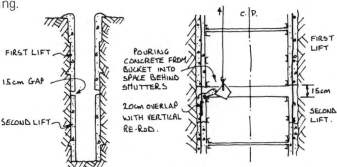

Pouring top of second lift.

77

The 15cm gap between lifts should be left open until the well has been excavated and lined to its full depth. Any settlement of each lift is most likely to have taken place by then, and the gaps can be filled with broken concrete bricks, or specially prepared H-shaped concrete blocks:—

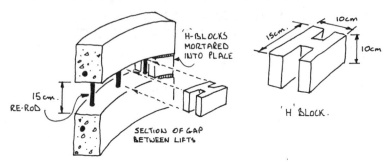

Filling gap between lifts with 'H' blocks.

The 10 x 10 x 15cm H-shaped blocks, which should have already been cast on the surface from a 1:3 cement:sand-mortar, are fitted between the vertical re-rods, and mortared soundly into place. You will find that it is easiest to do this after the shutters have been stripped away. These gaps can be used to attach the rising main pipe for a pump, or the supports for an access ladder.

The routine of digging and lining each lift is now continued until water is reached or until unstable ground conditions threaten the excavated well. Different procedures must be used in these cases; in difficult ground each lift can be as short as 65cm, 0.5 metres for one of the small shutters and 15cm to provide the pouring gap.

The most common difficulties in digging the well will be the occurrence of dry sand which flows into the excavation from the sides of the well, collapsing soils both wet and dry, or solid rock. Detailed descriptions of the methods you can use to tackle these conditions are given in Part III.

Experience has shown that in most wells, the greatest risk of collapse occurs from weak soil in the first few metres of the well. If this is made safe with the temporary lining or even the first lift, then it is sometimes possible, in firm soils, to excavate down until water is reached. The concrete lining, if it is needed to support the walls of the well, will then be

78

Photo 16   Levelling blocks upon which
the second set of shutters will rest.

Photo 17   Placing of re-rod begins.
Note the hooks and overlap.

Photo 18   Assembly of re-rod frame
before shutters are assembled.

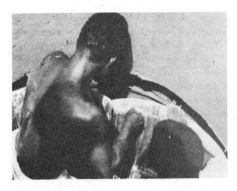

Photo 19   Fitting and bolting second
set of shutters.

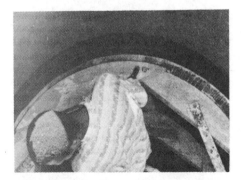

Photo 20   Centering and adjusting
shutters so that they are in line with
those above and below.

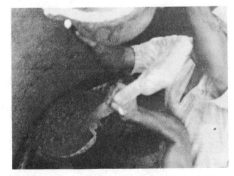

Photo 21   Pouring concrete through
gap above top set of shutters in lift.

poured up in one continuous lift with kerbs built in every 5 metres. Only you can judge if the ground is likely to be stable; the advantage of this method is that the well can be abandoned without waste of concrete if water is not found. Do not take risks, however, and if you are in doubt, line the well.

Finally, when water is reached, a strong curb is constructed in the lining at the bottom of the well to strengthen the end of the lining tube. It is of great importance at this stage of the work to auger a hole into the bottom of the well to discover what the aquifer is made of and if it is of shallow depth. If the aquifer is a shallow perched layer of water bearing strata, then the well must be sunk through this layer to a deeper aquifer.

CHAPTER 9 CAISSONING INTO AQUIFER AND CONSTRUCTION OF INTAKE — CONSTRUCTION STAGE 4

Below the water table the 'sink and line' method described above ceases to be practical, partly because of the difficulty of keeping the shaft clear of water to allow the sinkers to work, partly because the water seeping through the shaft wall will make the side unstable and will wash the cement out of the concrete placed behind the shutters.

If the aquifer is of consolidated material such as sandstone, fissured rock or hard laterite, it may be possible to continue sinking to the same diameter as before and either dispense with the lining or build it up using pre-cast concrete blocks. It is more usual to find that the water-bearing strata is of unstable sandy or gravelly material, in which case the method of construction recommended is caissoning.

The caisson lining is a concrete tube constructed at the bottom of the well inside the main lining. Its outside diameter is 1.20 metre (to allow it to be sunk inside the 1.3 metre internal diameter lining of the shaft) and its inside diameter is at least 90cm (to give room for one man to work inside). It is built up from the bottom of the well, and is then caused to sink under its own weight by excavating under its lower end. This is a slow process, only one sinker at a time being able to work within the tube, and the operation has to be constantly interrupted in order to pump or bail the interior free enough of water to permit excavation to continue. The deeper the tube penetrates below the water table the faster will the water enter, and the limit of sinking will be reached when it becomes impossible to keep the water level within the caisson down sufficiently for the sinker to continue working.

If the intake caisson is being constructed at the end of the dry season, when the water table is at its lowest, it may be possible to sink the tube low enough to ensure an adequate supply of water in the well throughout the year. If work is carried out at any other season it must be expected that the level will fall, possibly below the lower end of the caisson, in which case the well will run dry. To avoid this possibility the caisson tube is left projecting upward into the lining (the distance of the projection depending on the amount the water table is expected to fall) so that deepening can take place when the ground water is at its lowest. Deepening at the end of the dry season will involve excavation only, no further concreting or construction being necessary since the concrete caisson tube is there, waiting to descend.

The distance below the water table to which you can penetrate will be governed by the nature of the aquifer material as well as by the rate at which water can be pumped or bailed out. In consolidated aquifers you will be able to pump the well dry by buckets or other pumping devices without the risk of the aquifer material collapsing and running with the flow of water up into the well. If the aquifer is loose, however, you must not over-pump or caving will take place putting great stress on the linings, and you will risk losing the well altogether. A typical loose sandy aquifer will begin to cave in and flow with the water into the caisson when the water level has been pumped down about 2 metres. In this case, you will have to excavate under water, either by spade and scoop, or by using an orange peel grab.

There are three commonly used methods of constructing the caisson:—

a) Using reinforced concrete rings, precast on the surface.
b) Using reinforced concrete rings, poured at the bottom of the well.
c) Using precast concrete blocks, built on a cutting ring.

Of these methods the first is the most straightforward, and the quickest, and is described in detail below. It does, however, call for a headframe capable of carrying the weight of the precast caisson rings which weigh over 300kg; the frame described in Chapter 6 is quite suitable for the purpose, but if one of the 'makeshift' devices referred to in Part III is used it will be necessary to change the method of caisson construction.

Casting of caisson rings

The first stage is the casting of the rings, and this should be carried out as far in advance of need as possible, since the longer a period these rings have to cure and mature the stronger and more resistant to accidental damage during handling will they be. It is common practice to set aside part of the working site as a casting area, and to shade this area with a light grass roof (not only for the comfort of the workmen, but also to keep the newly cast rings out of direct sunlight). Casting of the rings can then be started while the upper part of the well shaft is being excavated, the disposition of the well team at that time being:—

2 sinkers, within the shaft

2 men operating the winch, removing excavated material

2 men mixing concrete and casting rings

1 headman, stationed by well mouth, operating hoist brake as required

Rings are cast, one at a time, in a mould with an internal diameter of 0.90 metres, an outside diameter of 1.20 metres, and a cylinder height of 0.5 metres. Four bolts are set at equal distances vertically into the cylinder wall; these bolts are made from 15mm diameter rod, each 1 metre long, the upper end being threaded to take a washer and nut, and having, near the lower end, a hole drilled to take a nail or other key to stop the bolt being pulled from the concrete under loading. The bolts are used to fasten the rings together when they are in the well.

Midway between the bolts four vertical holes are left in the cylinder wall. This is done by casting in four pieces of well-oiled pipe (or rod) about 20mm in diameter, and withdrawing these from the green concrete at least 12 hours, but not more than 24 hours after casting. If they are stuck fast, turn them with a 'Stillson' wrench and they should then slide out. The pipes must be smooth, straight, without dents or lips, or you will have trouble removing them.

To cast the ring the mould is assembled in the shade, the faces that will come into contact with the concrete are oiled, the bolts and the pieces of oiled pipe are held in place with the templates, and slips of wood are inserted to form recesses at the points where the nuts and washers will be fitted. The ring is now ready for concreting.

*Photo 22   Caisson ring mould 0.5 metre
deep — a) Interior sections. —
Upper Volta.*

*Photo 23   b) Exterior sections. —
Upper Volta.*

Photo 24   Caisson ring mould 0.5 metre deep — c) Making concrete rings. — India.

Photo 25   d) General view of caisson mould showing holes
through which re-rod is placed to make seepage holes.
Upper Volta.

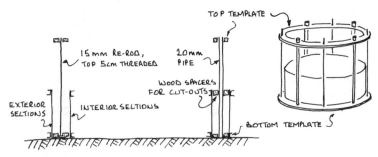

Setting up the caisson ring mould.

Whether the ring is to be made porous or solid will depend upon the nature of the aquifer expected. If the water bearing material is likely to be very fine sand, it is usually preferable to have the caisson wall solid and allow the water to enter through the bottom, where any inflow of aquifer solids can be controlled by a graded filter or base plug. In this case the mould will be filled with 1:2:4 concrete, poured some 10cm deep at a time, and compacted by tamping with a length of re-rod until the mould is full and all air bubbles have been removed.

If the aquifer is expected to be of decomposed rock, coarse sand or gravel it is usual to construct the caisson rings of porous material so that water can enter through the wall. There are two ways of doing this — using porous concrete, or using normal concrete into which seepage holes have been inserted.

Porous concrete, which consists of a dry mix of 1:1:4 (cement:sand:gravel), is the more straightforward method. The concrete should not be too wet, and instead of being tamped the mould is vibrated by banging with blocks of wood. The resultant rings require longer curing than normal concrete, are weaker and must consequently be handled with great care.

Seepage holes may be inserted in normal concrete rings by casting lengths of re-rod or wooden pegs (well oiled) into the rings and removing these before the concrete is completely set. There is more risk of fine sand being drawn from the aquifer through the seepage holes, but there is one con-structional advantage. If water enters at too great a rate during sinking seepage holes can be temporarily blocked off on the internal face with wooden bungs until the caisson has reached its final position:—

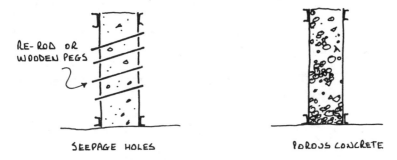

RE-ROD OR WOODEN PEGS

SEEPAGE HOLES

POROUS CONCRETE

Making the porous caisson rings.

Whatever the type of ring cast, it is important that sufficient concrete is mixed and the whole of the mould filled in a continuous operation. (A caisson ring 0.5 metres deep contains about 0.2 cubic metres of concrete). After tamping or vibrating the upper surface is trowelled smooth, the wooden spacer slips are removed, and the date of casting should be scratched into the trowelled surface. It is possible to remove the mould sections after 24 hours, but it is preferable to leave them in place for at least 3 days. In any case the newly cast ring should not be moved for 3 days, and if it is made of porous concrete it is better left for 1 week. As soon as the mould is removed the surface of the concrete should be protected from sunlight and 'cured' by covering with wet grass, sacking or leaves; this should continue for as long as possible, a week being considered the minimum curing period.

Lowering the caisson rings

When the 'in-situ' lining (described in Chapter 8 above) reaches the aquifer an extra deep curb is cast at the base of the lining and the exposed well floor is carefully levelled off to receive the lowest caisson ring. If the soil at the floor of the well is moist and soft, back fill with 30cm of gravel to provide a firm base upon which the caisson column may be constructed. The first ring to be lowered is the first one that was cast, and will be identified by the date scratched in the upper surface of the concrete. It should be rolled from the curing area to the side of the well, tipped upright so that the four bolts are projecting upward, and the stretcher is then fitted.

The stretcher to lift the rings is made from a strong piece of timber, 1.25 metres long and 15cm x 15cm square, with a U bolt attached to the middle for lifting, and two holes of 20mm diameter drilled 53cm away at either end to take the threaded rods. The stretcher is fitted over rods on opposite sides of the ring, lengths of water pipe are added on the rods, and the nuts and washers are screwed on to hold the stretcher hard against the concrete ring. The stretcher may be made from angle iron, but it must be strong enough to take the weight of the ring, or it will bend and distort the steel rods:—

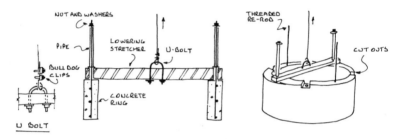

Lowering the pre-cast concrete rings.

Place logs or planks across the mouth of the shaft, fasten the main lowering rope to the U bolt in the centre of the stretcher, and with four men on the winch handles (one caisson ring 0.5 metre high weighs about 350kg) take the weight of the ring and manoeuvre it centrally over the well shaft.

When it is in the correct position raise it carefully by winching upwards a few centimetres, remove the planking from below and, very slowly to prevent swinging, lower it to the floor of the well. Before the rope and stretcher are uncoupled the ring must be checked both for position (precisely central within the lining) and for level. If necessary the ring must be lifted fractionally with the winch and adjusted with chocks; a very small error of level in the setting of this first ring will make subsequent ones very difficult to fit. The

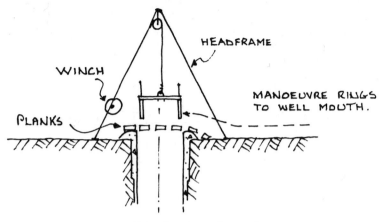

Take rings to well mouth.

stretcher is then removed and the four bolts left projecting upward without nuts on their upper ends.

The second ring is now lowered in the same manner as the first, but just before it reaches the projecting bolts of the first ring it is held by the winchmen and one of the sinkers (who has descended with the ring) turns it so that the holes in the second ring coincide with the bolts in the lower. The top edge of the lower ring is coated with about 10mm thick of mortar (1:4 cement and sand) and the upper one is lowered into place. The top, threaded, ends of the bolts of the first ring will just protrude into the recesses formed during casting in the upper edge of the second ring. Washers and nuts should be fitted (the level at the top of the ring should be checked and can be adjusted by tightening or loosening these nuts). Not until this has been done should the stretcher and rope be removed from the bolts of the second ring. The sinker, who is adjusting the alignment of the rings before they are finally lowered and screwed down, should under no circumstances put his fingers into the gap between the suspended ring and the lower ring; if the winch slips, he is likely to have his fingers crushed by the weight of the descending ring.

It is a useful precaution to pour a little cement slurry around the bolts before fitting washers and nuts.

The third and subsequent rings are fitted in the same manner. When four or five have been fixed together the head-

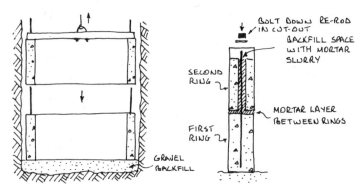

Connecting the rings.

man descends into the caisson and probes the bottom with a length of sharpened re-rod to see whether the ground is clear of boulders and of reasonably constant hardness. One danger has to be watched for with a telescoped caisson — the risk that soft ground below the bottom ring will give way under the weight when excavation starts. This can happen if a band of hard material or boulders halts the descent and suddenly yields. Provided that there are sufficient rings to the upper end of the caisson this will not matter, but it is most important that the topmost ring is not allowed to leave the lining otherwise the well may have to be abandoned. Downward slips of as much as 1.5 metres are not uncommon, so it is a wise precaution never to have less than five or six rings of 0.5 metre depth each within the shaft lining before excavation starts.

Sinking the caisson

Excavation takes place inside the caisson in the following way. A hole is dug first in th centre of the well, and cut back in layers all around the sides towards the ring. Take care with this excavation as digging away too much on one side may cause the caisson to sink out of line. When you have cut back far enough, the caisson should begin to sink slowly under its own weight.

Sinking should continue until the water becomes too deep, or you are satisfied that the well will yield enough water. A water pump to drain the well will allow you to sink the caisson several extra metres deeper into the aquifer, but

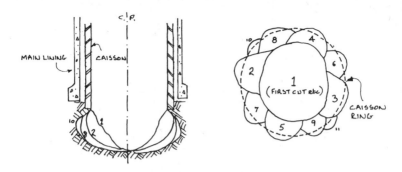

Stages of cutting under caisson.

unless great care is used there is the risk of caving, sideways movement of the caisson or collapse of the aquifer. Alternatively, you can leave the final aquifer sinking until the end of the dry season when the water table has fallen to its lowest level.

When the caisson has been sunk to its required depth a base plug is installed at the base of the well. The plug is an essential part of the well as it prevents the aquifer material from flowing up into the well if the well is over pumped. The plug can be made of porous concrete pre-cast on the surface and lowered down the well, or from layers of sand and gravel:—

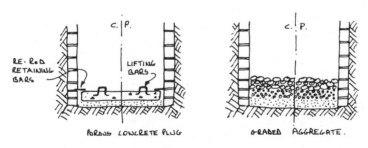

Making the base plug.

The plug is pre-cast at the wellhead from porous concrete of 1:1:4 (cement:sand:gravel), reinforced with re-rod. The re-rod retaining bars, which are only necessary in a well sunk into fine shifting sand, can be removed if the plug has to be lifted out during well deepening operations.

91

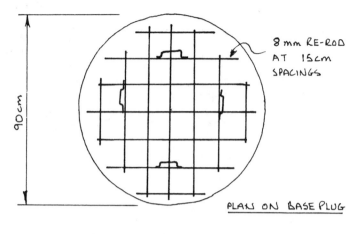

8 mm RE-ROD
AT 15cm
SPACINGS

90cm

PLAN ON BASE PLUG

LIFTING HOOKS

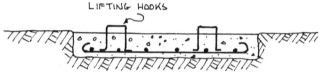

Section of base plug cast in mould dug into the ground.

The sand and gravel filter is made from layers of graded sand and gravel which are raked level at the well base. This type of filter is probably the simplest to install; it can be improved greatly by a thin porous concrete slab resting on top.

After the plug or filter has been installed, the space outside the caisson (between it and the upper lining) should be filled with small gravel. On no account should mortar or concrete be used here; the caisson must not be rigidly fixed to the shaft lining above.

CHAPTER 10   CONSTRUCTION OF WELLHEAD —
CONSTRUCTION STAGE 5

The wellhead consists of a reinforced concrete head wall, 1 metre high, 15cm thick, with a gently sloping concrete apron at least 2 metres wide, to carry away spilled water. The wall prevents animals and people from falling down the well and provides a mounting for pumps. The concrete apron provides a firm base for the well users to walk on and rest their buckets and it carries away spilled and polluted water. Many water related diseases are transmitted by badly cared for wells and the drainage apron is of great importance. The spilled water should be led away in a drainage ditch into a soakaway pit.

In Part I of this manual we have included a detailed section on wells and health. We must emphasise that a polluted well will spread disease amongst all of the water users and the only completely reliable way of preventing the well water from being contaminated from the surface is to seal the top of the well; an open well is always an open target for rubbish especially from small boys. You should endeavour to educate the well users in the need for care and cleanliness in using the well. One of the main reasons for choosing open wells in preference to the small diameter bore holes however, is that simple water lifting devices, such as a rope and bucket, may be used.

To make the wellhead, proceed as follows: Break up the weak mortar layer around the stub wall of the main lining and bend the re-rods up into a vertical position. Fix and tie four horizontal circles of 8mm re-rod to the vertical re-rods and tie to each a re-rod bent into an elbow shape as shown overleaf. These right-angle bars will provide reinforcement for the concrete apron.

Bend and secure eight circles of re-rod around the apron bars, and fix the main lining shutters in place over the well.

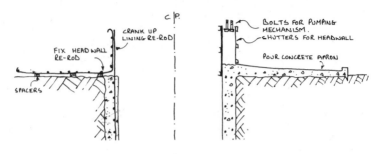

Building up wellhead.

At this stage you should already have decided what sort of pumping equipment the people in your area will be able to build and maintain. This determines the sort of mountings that will be needed on the wellhead. The hardwood rollers shown opposite have been very successful and to mount these pairs of bolts are set into the concrete wall for each side of the roller.

The outside shutter for the wall may be either made specially for the purpose or may be built up out of scrap wood. It should have an internal radius of 80cm giving a final collar wall thickness of 15cm. Using the normal 1:2.5:5 concrete mix, pour the apron slab first, allow it to set, and fix the collar wall shutters. Mount the assembled rollers and bearings in their correct positions on the top of the shutters and fill the space with concrete. Tamp the concrete in the usual way and cover with wet sacks or plastic for at least 7 days to give it time to cure.

Finally, strip away the shuttering and clean up the well site. Any rough spots on the wellhead can be filled in by hand using a trowel and sand:cement mortar.

The edge of the apron should be formed with a low curb all round, except for a few centimetres at the lowest point of the circumference. From here a ditch, lined with mortar, should lead any water spilled on the apron to a soakaway (a pit filled with broken blocks or other hard rubble) a few metres from the apron edge. Before finally trowelling the surface of the apron to a smooth finish, wait until the concrete is beginning to set and pour a bucket or two of water over it to make sure that the slope is correct and all spillage drains away reasonably quickly.

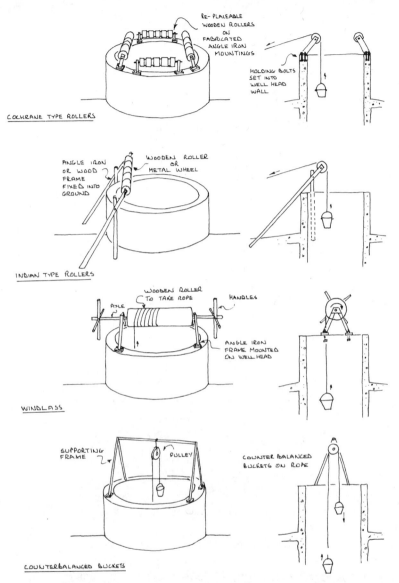

RE-PLACEABLE
WOODEN ROLLERS
ON
FABRICATED
ANGLE IRON
MOUNTINGS

HOLDING BOLTS
SET INTO
WELL HEAD
WALL

COCHRANE TYPE ROLLERS

ANGLE IRON
OR WOOD
FRAME
FIXED INTO
GROUND

WOODEN ROLLER
OR
METAL WHEEL

INDIAN TYPE ROLLERS

WOODEN ROLLER
TO TAKE ROPE

AXLE

HANDLES

ANGLE IRON
FRAME MOUNTED
ON WELL HEAD

WINDLASS

SUPPORTING
FRAME

PULLEY

COUNTER BALANCED
BUCKETS ON ROPE

COUNTERBALANCED BUCKETS

Simple water lifting equipment for hand dug wells.

A somewhat more elaborate, though still relatively inexpensive wellhead is widely used in Northern Nigeria and elsewhere for village installations. Beside each set of rollers

95

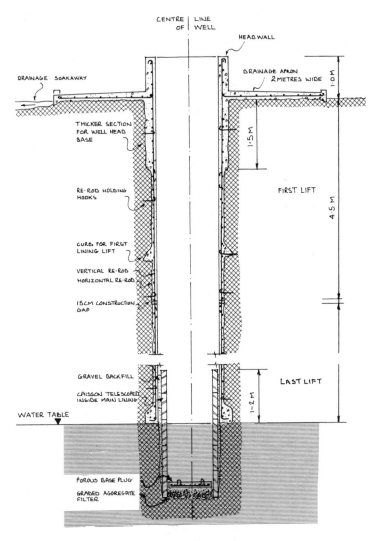

Cross section through finished well.

is a shallow basin, built of concrete blocks plastered to a smooth finish. At the bottom of each basin slope is a short length of galvanised pipe that projects through the wall at such a height that a pot, kerosene tin, or other container can be placed on the apron below the open end. Water is drawn by rope and bucket and tipped into the basin from which it runs into the pot without spillage, splashing or waste. This allows the use of containers that are almost completely closed (and therefore more hygienic for carrying) such as a kerosene container with the top intact except for a small pouring hole or a narrow necked gourd or jar which would otherwise be impossible to fill directly from a lifting bucket.

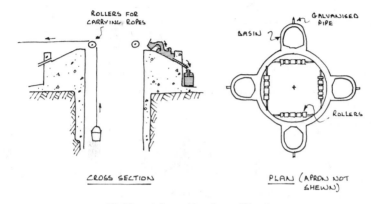

CROSS SECTION   PLAN (APRON NOT SHEWN)

Wellhead from Northern Nigeria.
See also photographs on page 103.

If a mechanical pump of some sort is available and the well users understand and are able to maintain and repair it, the well may be sealed with a concrete slab. This will prevent surface contamination, and reduce the risks of polluted well water to a level similar to that expected from a sealed tube well. The 15cm thick reinforced concrete slab may be cast in a mould excavated into the ground in the same way used to construct the caisson base plug. It is reinforced with 8mm re-rod at 15cm spacings, and has a circular opening 50 x 50cm in diameter to allow access for cleaning the well:—

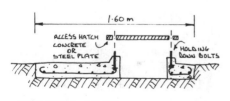

CAST SLAB IN GROUND

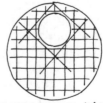

PLAN VIEW SHOWING DIAGONAL RE-ROD.

Construction of wellhead slab.

Because of the stresses set up around the access hatch, extra re-rods are tied into place diagonally with the main re-rods. The access hatch is provided with a concrete lip at the top to prevent spilt water from draining into the well and the hatch bolts are cast into the lip. The upper surface is also trowelled to give a sloping surface.

The wellhead cover should not be built until the water pump has been chosen and is ready on the site. It is easiest to erect the pump with its mounting bolts in the mould, provide a cut out in the slab for the rising main pipe (making sure it is large enough to allow the pump body to be withdrawn from the well) and then cast the concrete. The pump is removed when the concrete has cured, to allow the slab to be lifted into place over the well.

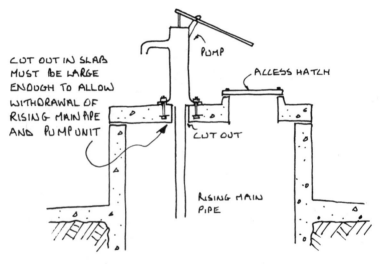

Wellhead with slab and pump.

In many cases where the pump has broken down and the well users are not able to repair it, the slab has simply been levered off, and the traditional rope and bucket used. This re-opens the mouth of the well to contaminated matter, and the cost of the pump and slab is wasted. For this reason it is essential to make sure that either the well users understand how to look after the pump, or that a responsible local authority will maintain it.

98

CHAPTER 11 DISINFECTION OF WELL BEFORE USE

Preventing contaminated wastes from entering the well water is a more effective strategy in the long term for rural areas than disinfecting the water before it is used. Disinfection can be expensive, needs regular attention and the treated well water may be unpalatable to many people unless the dosage is strictly controlled.

Disinfection is however, essential after your well has been constructed. The well should be thoroughly cleaned and sterilised with a strong disinfectant and allowed to stand for several days before use; this will kill any bacteria and parasites that may have entered the well or pumping system during construction. Open, hand dug wells are particularly at risk to contamination during construction by well diggers, and the walls should be thoroughly scrubbed with disinfectant.

The most easily obtainable and safe disinfectant is a solution made up by mixing household bleach with water to give a chlorine solution:—

i. Mix 2 litres of ordinary bleach in 35 litres of water. For a hand dug well, scrub the sides with this solution then pour the remainder into the well. To disinfect any pumping equipment, pour the solution directly into the well and pump until the chlorine odour appears at the well head; re-circulate the water back into the well for at least an hour.

ii. Mix a similar solution and pour this into the well, allowing it to stand overnight.

iii. Pump the well to waste until the odour of chlorine disappears; the chlorine may persist for a week or more, depending on the volume of water in the well and the pumping rate. The remaining chlorine in the well will disappear slowly in time as it oxidises.

Disinfecting the well immediately after construction will

not keep the well water sterilised for more than a few days. Contamination that enters the well after this sterilising dose will not be destroyed. If you have doubts about the purity of the well water then you have no alternative but to attempt to treat the water before it is used. Water treatment, either in the well or at the surface, is beyond the scope of this manual.

CHAPTER 12 SAFETY MEASURES IN WELL CONSTRUCTION

The dangers of working in well diggings and the accidents that can occur are perhaps difficult to forsee if you have no previous experience in this type of work; well excavation and construction should always be under the supervision of someone who at least understands what can go wrong. Try and visit well sites under construction, and talk with experienced diggers. The most common causes of accidents are poor equipment, material falling down the well, the collapse of the well, and occasionally asphyxiation from gases. The deeper the well, the greater the risk of accidents. However, if you adopt standard safety measures and make sure that all of your workmen understand what can go wrong, and use their common sense, then you will have little trouble.

a) Checking equipment

All equipment, ropes, pulleys, head frames, lifting devices, ladders, etc., must be checked at the start of each day and thoroughly examined to see that they have adequate strength. All ropes should be handled foot by foot, as minor damage to the strands of a rope can quickly worsen causing the rope to break when under load; knots and joins should also be carefully examined.

A common danger spot is the handle at the end of the concrete lowering rope. It is usual to tie a short piece of wood to the rope end to ensure a firm grip if the rope itself becomes wet and slippery, and if this handle slips out or the knot becomes untied the bucket of concrete (or other load) that is being lowered will fall on to the men working below. The handle itself should be strong, and should be attached by a double clove hitch and two bulldog clips in the centre. The knot and clips should be periodically checked during working. All equipment should be properly assembled before the commencement of work and approved by someone who has experience of the loads that will be put upon it. In particular the head frame should be erected as if it is to stay in place as a permanent structure. Makeshift head frames, hemp or leather ropes, buckets for lifting water and baskets for lifting excavated materials, are cheap to make and buy if you are only planning to construct one or two wells. But these are inherently weaker than purpose made proven equipment, which should be used if you have a larger programme. The purpose made equipment improves the speed and safety of construction, giving a cheaper and sounder well. If you use makeshift equipment you will increase the risk of accidents.

All kibbles and buckets should have a loop in the centre of the handle to prevent tilting sideways, and should have the handle hinged at or near the top rim, so that if they catch a projection while being raised or lowered they will not accidentally discharge their contents.

The headman, or someone responsible, should always be stationed at the well mouth during raising or lowering of buckets, ready to order the men at the upper end of the rope to cease hauling and hold firm if the load jams or starts swinging.

Two apparently minor, but relatively common, causes of accident are the following. Fingers can be trapped (and in some cases actually severed) at the point where the rope passes over the headframe pulley or on to the winch. Adjustments should never be made by hand while the rope is under load. Shovels used for concrete mixing can become razor sharp with wear on the mixing tray; when two men are mixing together the shovel of one can inflict a serious wound on the feet or ankles of his fellow.

The safest way of ascending or descending a deep shaft is on a bosun's chair, either purpose made (see Chapter 18) or consisting of a strong piece of timber knotted to the rope in the same way as the handle at the upper end. Putting one foot in a bucket and holding the rope with one hand is probably the least safe.

b) Preventing materials and people from falling into the well

Hand rails or fencing should if possible be erected around the site to prevent unnecessary access to the well, especially

102

Photo 26   Cattle Watering Trough — Northern Nigeria.

Photo 27   Nigerian Wellhead with Wooden Rollers — Northern Nigeria.

Photo 28   Nigerian Wellhead with Shallow Basins — Northern Nigeria.

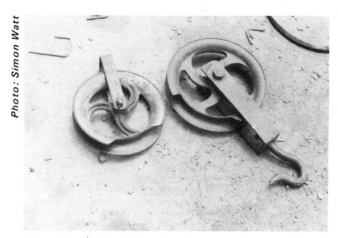

Photo 29   Badly designed equipment is sure to cause accidents --- Cheap lifting tackle will soon break under the strain.

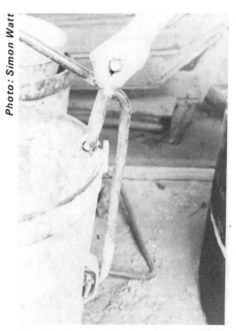

Photo 30   Badly designed kibble with safety handle. The kibble is held in the middle, not at the top rim; if safety handle is accidently lifted as kibble is lowered, then kibble will tip its contents.

Photo 31   Showing how safety catch is lifted to release handle.

Photo: Ian Mathie

Photo 32   Safe method of entry into well on simple bosun's chair made from a piece of timber. — Upper Volta.

Photo 33   Unsafe way of leaving well — many accidents are caused this way. — India.

at night or when the area is unattended. The upstanding lip built at the start of construction around the top of the well is designed to prevent shovels, stones, planks, etc., from being accidently kicked down down the well shaft. In any case, all loose equipment that is not being used during the construction operations should be stored away from the wellhead. Shovels that have become sharpened while mixing concrete will be especially lethal if dropped down the well.

When the well sinkers are working from ladders, bosun chairs or scaffold planks, it is advisable that they wear a rope attached around their waists, made fast and controlled from the surface.

We have already emphasised the need to use sound equipment in well construction work. Your well sinkers will work with greater confidence if they are sure that bucket loads of concrete or excavated material will not spill and fall down the well shaft onto them. Safety helmets should always be worn down the well.

c) Well collapse

It is not advisable to construct a well in lifts deeper than 5m without a well lining or temporary shutter being put into place. The lining or shutter should be made secure, and checked at intervals for stability; great care should be taken with temporary cribbing which will be withdrawn when construction has been completed. You risk your life and the lives of your well sinkers if you try to dig a deep well without a lining, although in most cases collapse occurs when the loose surface layers fall into the well. The temporary lining built at the top of the well will prevent this.

d) Dangerous gases

In certain types of ground, gases may be released that can be dangerous (and even fatal) to the sinkers. This condition is fortunately not very common, but should be watched for especially where sinking is taking place in a new area of unknown geology. The gases may be suffocating, explosive or poisonous, and will generally (though by no means always) give notice of their presence by a musty or foul smell. In deep shafts (say over 50 metres) the sinkers themselves will consume oxygen and exhale carbon dioxide to an extent that will make the atmosphere unbearable without some form of ventilation. As the depth increases sinkers can only work for short periods at a time; even with ventilation their output will drop after about an hour, and changing places with those working at the surface regularly is a good precaution to take.

Some ventilation takes place every time a bucket or basket is lifted to the surface, and a simple way to increase this effect is to raise and lower a few times rapidly a basket or bundle of twigs. Alternatively air may be pumped down from the surface by a device such as this:—

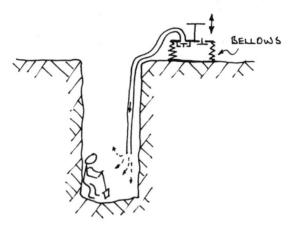

Simple bellows blowing fresh air into well.

The practice of lowering a petrol or diesel driven dewatering pump down a well shaft during construction or maintenance can quickly build up a dangerous concentration of toxic gases and is not recommended. If it is done, no one should be allowed to enter the shaft until it has been thoroughly ventilated and the quality of the air tested by lowering a lighted candle. In some places a caged bird is used to confirm that the air is fit to breathe, a custom that cannot be commended because of its cruelty, but is better than risking the lives of the sinkers.

Similar conditions may be produced when explosives are used for rock blasting within a well. All explosives give off some toxic gas; locally manufactured compounds are usually more dangerous than those prepared for commercial purposes. Again no one should be allowed to descend until the shaft has been thoroughly purged of all poisonous fumes.

e) Sanitation and the well sinkers

The health risks to the future users of the well resulting from defecation in the well by the well sinkers must be very carefully explained. All men working down a well must leave the well to defecate — a single man who is a carrier of typhoid can start an epidemic by contaminating the water supply source, even though the well is to be disinfected on completion. Defecation in the well must be absolutely forbidden.

f) Attendance at the wellhead and signals

Whenever men are working down a well someone must be in close attendance at the top either to help them out or to keep a close watch on activities below in case of accidents.

A system of signalling should be adopted which is clearly understood by everyone constructing the well; this is for the safe control of lowering and hoisting of men, materials, spoil, tools, etc. This system can involve tugging a rope, making loud noises, or by flashing a light. It is suggested that the following code of signals be used:—

One signal	—	stop
Two signals	—	lower
Three signals	—	hoist
Four signals	—	hoist personnel.

In addition, an audible personal alarm signal such as a whistle, is recommended which can be quickly operated in an emergency.

We cannot emphasise strongly enough the need for thoroughly understood and practiced safety measures. Good safety practice quickly becomes normal routine. It is not worth taking risks with the lives of your well diggers in order to save a small amount of money or construction time.

PART III ALTERNATIVE TECHNIQUES AND MATERIALS

CHAPTER 13   WELL SINKING UNDER DIFFICULT
SOIL CONDITIONS

The Methods described in Part II are suitable for use in a wide variety of soils, but there are certain conditions where special precautions have to be taken and different techniques adopted. Some of these are described in this chapter.

Rock

The most obvious obstacle to the hand digging of wells is hard bedrock, such as granite, basalt or hard limestone. It is possible, but laborious, to penetrate such strata by traditional methods, which include opening up natural fissures by hammer and wedges. In general bedrock without such fissures will not contain water anyway and there is little point in trying to sink further when such solid rock is encountered.

Traditional sinkers have been known to break up hard rock by lighting fires on the surface to heat the top layer which is then suddenly cooled by pouring on cold water — the rapid change of temperature causing the rock surface to split and craze. Today the only methods considered practicable involve the use of compressed air tools or explosives, both of which are outside the immediate scope of this manual. Compressed air tools are safer to use than explosives but the motor powered compressors require skilled maintenance and control if they are not to increase the cost of the wells to an unacceptable degree.

Collapsing soils

One of the disadvantages of the sink-and-line method of well sinking is the necessity of leaving a length of the shaft wall unsupported for a time during construction. In very firm ground there may be little hazard of collapse and the well can sometimes be excavated from the surface down the aquifer in one single lift quite safely. It is wiser even where the wall appears to be quite stable to restrict the height of each lift to a maximum of 5 metres as described in Part II. There are types of soil where it is dangerous to leave even this length unsupported. Only experience will guide you to a decision but it is always safer to line in shorter lifts if there is any doubt, such as might be aroused by cracking, crumbling, swelling or sideways movement of the unsupported shaft wall. In extreme cases each lining lift can be made as short as 1 metre, or even 0.5 metre. The method of excavation, trimming and erecting the re-rods and lining shutters for these short lifts follows exactly the same method described for the long 5 metre lifts, except that the re-rod is given a 30cm elbow bend at the bottom of the shutters and pegged to the well bottom:—

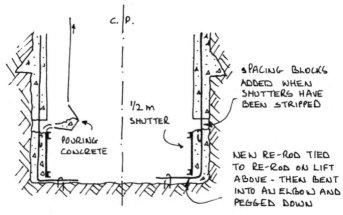

Pouring 0.5 metre lining lifts.

This elbow bend is straightened up after the concrete has set, to tie onto the re-rod in the lift below. Bending the re-rod can work-harden and weaken the steel, and if you are able to push the re-rod 30cm into the bottom of the well then this is preferable. Remember to use extra re-rods for crumbling soils, up to 30 vertical re-rods, and 4 horizontal re-rods per metre depth. (See Chapter 8.)

The excavation for the short lifts must be the depth of the shutters plus about 15cm, giving room for the concrete to be poured behind the shutters. The spacing blocks are then mortared into place in the gap; leave the final plastering and pointing until the shutters have been stripped.

114

These short lifts are taken down until the ground becomes stable enough to stand up on its own in longer lifts, or until the aquifer is reached when the usual caisson sinking method is adopted.

Dry sliding sand

A type of soil sometimes encountered is a loose, dry sand, often called 'sugar' sand, which will slide under its own weight. It usually occurs in pockets in otherwise firm sedimentary soils, and its potentially dangerous behaviour is often only seen after the well shaft has been excavated through it. If it can be identified as soon as it is met in the bottom of the well it is easy to deal with — just keep it continually wet while excavating through it, and line in half-metre lifts.

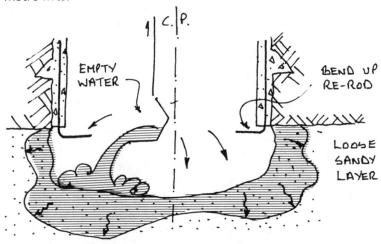

Wetting dry sand at bottom of well.

What is more likely to happen is that the sand will contain some moisture and will appear quite firm when first encountered. Excavation continues normally so that the well cuts through the 'sugar' layer which then becomes part of the shaft wall. Only after it has been exposed to the atmosphere for some hours does it begin to slide out of the wall.

Action should be taken quickly since if the pocket is of appreciable size a serious situation may develop, with the risk of caving and collapse of the shaft wall above. The usual way

115

of dealing with the situation is to assemble lining shutters in the well, set them around the shaft and sink them as though they were caisson rings, then pour water outside them until the surrounding sand is thoroughly saturated all round. Strip the shutters, trim the wall to shape and line it with concrete in short lifts; do not attempt to excavate for curbs near the sandy section of wall. Make the concrete wetter than usual, with a rather higher proportion of cement, so that it will soak into and bind the sugar sand. Lifts should not be more than 1 metre in depth (0.5 metre may be preferable) and should be built as described above for collapsing soils. Shutters should be left in place to support the concrete for at least 7 days after lining.

The short lengths between lifts are built up using mortar and concrete spacing blocks. It will usually be found necessary, before finally pointing the blocks after the shutters have been stripped, to pour more water through the blocks and have the ground behind thoroughly wetted before finishing off with cement mortar.

If when the shutters are stripped before the final trimming and lining, the sand in the wall (where it has been soaked) still looks unstable it is better to change from lining to caissoning for the remainder of the well.

Wet sand

There is a condition known as 'running sand' in which water flows through a sand bed with such velocity that the material of the aquifer flows with it. This condition is not often met with; if it is it can be dealt with by caissoning. What is more usual is a bed of saturated sand that is unstable because of its water content — this is often mis-called 'running' sand. When it forms part of the aquifer that is to be tapped there is no difficulty; caissoning methods used below the water table will cope with the instability and prevent undue sand movement that could lead to aquifer collapse.

Sometimes, however, a well will pass through one or more 'perched' aquifers above the main water bearing strata. The material of these aquifers may be waterlogged sand, but because the area is restricted they may constitute too small a reservoir to be worth tapping. In section they are as illustrated opposite:

116

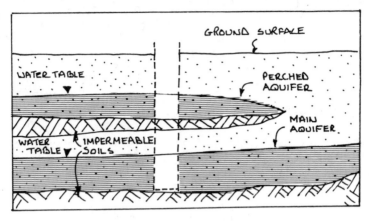

Perched aquifer above main aquifer.

The well sinker will not see them like this, of course. He will encounter the water table and aquifer, perhaps at a higher level than he expected, and he may be deceived into thinking that he has reached the main ground water reservoir. If he is unwise enough to install an intake caisson at this level he may find himself with a good-yielding well that runs dry after a short period of use.

The first thing to find out, then, is whether the aquifer reached is the main one or not. If it is perched it will probably be of small thickness and will be underlain by an impermeable layer (usually of clay, silt, or shale, but sometimes of hard rock). Probing through the bottom of the well with sharpened lengths of re-rod, or augering a hole downward will give a clue. Sinking the unlined shaft as far as possible into the aquifer and trying to bail it dry will provide an idea as to how much water is likely to be obtained.

If the aquifer is judged to be a perched one sinking will have to continue through and below it to reach the main water table. It may be desired to tap the aquifer to augment the yield of the well, or it may be that its quality is poor, or that the quantity available is insufficient to be worthwhile exploiting, but whichever decision is reached it will be necessary to block off the upper water during the sinking of the remainder of the well to avoid flooding the shaft. This means that caissoning must be adopted through the critical strata.

The simplest solution is to change over to caissoning methods and to continue these down until the main aquifer is reached. If this distance is expected to be more than a few metres there are disadvantages in this course of action — the diameter of the well is reduced, only one man can work at a time, the long caisson may go out of vertical or may become jammed and refuse to sink.

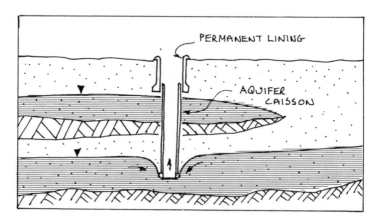

Caisson sinking through perched aquifer to main aquifer.

Because of these considerations the following procedure may be usefully adopted. When you have reached the top aquifer, and explored its thickness with probes or auger, complete the concrete lining with a bottom curb about 1.5 metres above the water level, leaving the re-rod hanging below in the usual way.

A caisson lining is built using extra reinforcement and flattened sheet iron from oil drums etc., laid against the soil walls and outside the 1.30 metre diameter shutters. The bottom of the lining should be given a cutting edge, and the over length re-rod is bent up the inside of the shutters.

Do not for the moment attach the re-rod at the top of the caisson to the re-rod of the lining above.

Now excavate carefully inside the caisson, leaving the shutters in place, and when the caisson has sunk 0.5 metre, tie on short lengths of re-rod, bolt on the 0.5 metre shutter, pour the concrete, and continue sinking after the concrete has set. The flat sheet iron behind the caisson lining prevents skin

118

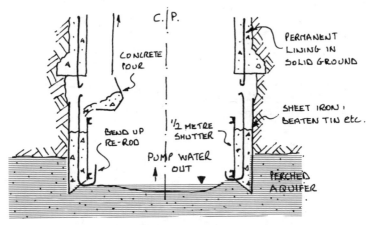

Sinking the caisson through the perched aquifer.

friction being developed during casting with the walls of the well. You will speed the work up if you use quick setting cement but special precautions are required.

Continue sinking the caisson 0.5 metre at a time in this way, leaving the shutters in place to support the caisson, until the impermeable lower layer is reached. From here on, excavate very carefully and slowly making the caisson as tight a fit as possible in the impermeable layer. When you have sunk about 0.5 metre into the impermeable layer, tie the caisson re-rod to the lining re-rod, and complete the lining. This will allow the caisson to hang when you excavate deeper:—

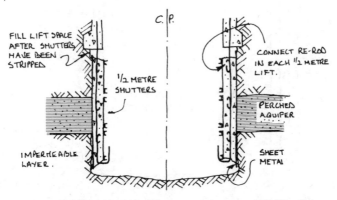

Excavate into impermeable layer and connect to lift above.

119

Allow the concrete at least a week to cure, then excavate again 65cm below the caisson cutting edge. Water will undoubtedly pour out from behind the caisson and you must block up the holes by stuffing cement bags into the gap, or better still, small plastic bags filled with quick setting plaster or cement. If the flow is not great, puddled clay may serve the purpose if rammed well home.

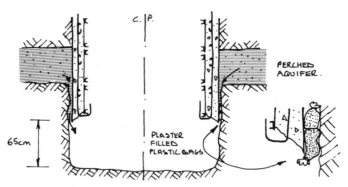

Stopping water flow with plaster filled plastic bags.

If you can stem the flow of water from behind the caisson cut out a curb into the sides of the impermeable layer and fix new re-rod down to the bottom of the excavation. Bend down the caisson re-rod, tie it to the re-rod below, and set a

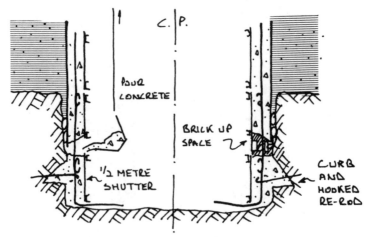

Casting lining into impermeable layer.

0.5 metre shutter in the usual way. Backfill the shutter with concrete, making sure that the curb is filled, and brick up the gap.

If, however, you have difficulty stemming the flow of water, do not bother with a curb in this lift but concentrate on pouring the lining and bricking up the gap. You can then build a curb in the next 1 metre of lining below.

The perched aquifer will now be sealed behind the caisson lining, which is joined to the permanent lining both below and above the perched aquifer. Remove all the shutters and sinking can now continue using the dig down—build up methods already described.

The water from the perched aquifer can make a useful contribution to the yield of the completed well. If you are satisfied that this water is not contaminated from the surface, or does not contain excessive concentrations of minerals, then you can allow it to enter the well through seepage holes.

If the caisson section completely seals the perched aquifer the pressure of water may build up and cause the caisson to collapse. On the other hand cases have been recorded where the water flowing through the seepage holes has carried with it the loose sand, causing caving behind the lining which then collapses.

You can overcome this difficulty by casting many short lengths of plastic tubing into the walls of the caisson. These are sealed by the shutter during sinking, but will open up when the shutter is removed. They can be cleaned out or even pulled out of the caisson lining to leave narrow seepage holes:—

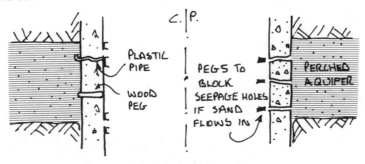

Tapping perched aquifer.

These holes can be plugged by wooden pegs until the well is completed, after which the pegs are withdrawn to allow water to enter. If the entering water then carries sand or silt there is a danger of caving behind the shaft wall, and it will probably be safer to return the plugs, or to stop off the holes permanently with mortar.

CHAPTER 14 ALTERNATIVE MATERIALS AND METHODS FOR WELL LINING

The materials and methods described in Part II for well sinking and lining have been selected for detailed description because they have been proved in practice to be safe, efficient and economical. They are especially applicable where a number of wells have to be constructed, where the cost of equipment can be spread over a number of sites, where the skill of the sinkers can be built up with experience to pay dividends in the shape of lower costs of subsequent construction.

There are undoubtedly circumstances that will, in some instances, call for a different approach and an attempt has been made in this chapter to describe some alternatives and conditions that will make these applicable.

First is the case where only one well is to be built and lined with reinforced concrete and where the speed of construction is not important. By using the method of 'dig-a-metre, line-a-metre' (the name is self-explanatory) it is possible to operate with makeshift lifting tackle instead of a specially made steel headframe, with a single set of shutters or even no shutters at all. Progress is necessarily slow because each metre lined must be allowed to reach its set strength before the work starts on the next section.

The second alternative described is known as 'steining', in which lifts of brick or masonry are supported on temporary props while the section below is being excavated. This is a very old method, largely superseded today by the cheaper and quicker reinforced concrete lining but still used in some places where bricks or building stone are plentiful and there are local skills in laying these materials.

Some notes are also given on the use and limitations of alternative materials such as timber or bamboo for well lining.

a) Dig-a-metre, pour-a-metre using improvised equipment

The following substitute headframe is widely used in West Africa in single or isolated self-help well projects. It can be made strong enough to perform most of the functions of a standard headframe but it should not be used for precast caisson rings which (constructed to the pattern given in Part II) weigh some 350kg each. It must be remembered that it is not just the deadweight of the load that has to be considered; a jerking movement during lowering or a temporary jamming of the rope in a pulley may impose a load equivalent to several times the weight of the object being raised or lowered.

The headframe

This is cheap to make from local materials, and can carry several lifting pulleys at the same time; after construction it may also be used as a frame to raise water with a rope and bucket.

It is erected in the following way:--

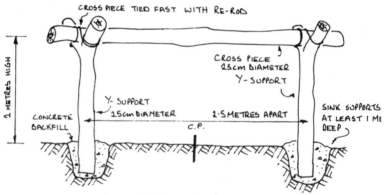

Setting up headframe.

The base of the Y-supports are lowered into holes dug at least 1 metre into the ground, and the space around the supports back-filled with a lean concrete mix. This will hold the head frame firmly in place. The Y-supports and the crosspiece must be straight, free from termites, at least 25cm thick and with no trace of decay. The crosspiece is bound to the Y-supports by re-rod to avoid any danger of the head frame working loose. The headframe must be able to take a load of

124

at least 250kg, to give a safety margin when heavy loads are lifted.

The lifting tackle

Two pulleys are attached securely with re-rod to the cross-piece, one pulley carries the men into the well, the other carries the excavated soil, lining moulds, concrete, etc. It is best to use gated pulleys that hold the lifting ropes in place. Poor quality pulleys will soon break and cause accidents.

The ropes must be strong and without defects. Locally made ropes are often used, but you should reduce the risks of accidental breakage by purchasing sound, commercial hemp ropes. Steel strand ropes, such as are used with the standard headframe, are safer but more difficult to handle without risk of injury to the well diggers' hands.

The brake post

The brake post is set 1 metre into the ground in concrete about 5 metres away from the well, and facing the crosspiece. The lifting ropes are wrapped around the brake post when the well sinkers and heavy weights are being lowered, to control the rate of descent. The brake post should be round and smooth.

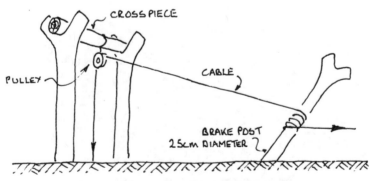

The brake post acting as friction clutch.

Reinforced concrete well construction using no shutters or moulds

Occasionally, you will need to make perhaps just one shallow well in good soil, where you have no shutters available. Many

*Photo 34   View of Well Site Using Improvised Headframe
— View of wellhead. Notice the man on the rope by the
brakepost on the left, the aggregate stockpiles, the cutting
ring mould and aquifer caisson blocks. — Upper Volta.*

*Photo 35   Lowering man down the well. The improvised
headframe is made from local timber. — Upper Volta.*

wells have been successfully made using the methods described below but we cannot recommend them; the cost of lining shutters and moulds is usually far outweighed by the benefits they bring in ease and efficiency of construction.

The well excavation work is set up in exactly the same way as described in Part II; the well is dug and trimmed using the plumbing rods, plumb line and mattocks, to a depth of 1 or 2 metres. The walls are splashed with cement slurry to prevent them from crumbling and when this is dry a 1:4 (cement:sand) mortar is plastered onto the walls with a trowel or wooden float, to a thickness of 3cm. Start work at the bottom and work your way up to the top of the well.

Give this mortar a few hours to harden, then install and fix horizontal and vertical reinforcement of the same size and numbers as recommended in the standard method; peg this re-rod flat against the plaster with hooks pushed into the walls, and bind the rods together with soft iron tie wire.

A second 3cm thick layer of mortar is trowelled on in the same way as the first layer, covering the reinforcement completely and, in effect, embedding it in the centre of a mortar wall 6cm thick. At all costs the two 3cm layers must be bonded together; if any dirt has fallen on to the first layer it must be washed off before the second is applied. If more than a few hours have elapsed the surface of the first layer should be scored and roughened to make a close bond. The wall is now covered with plastic sheeting or damp sacks for

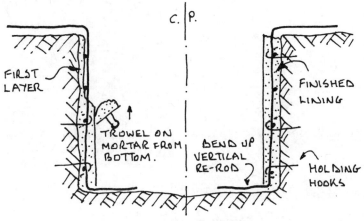

Lining without a shutter.

127

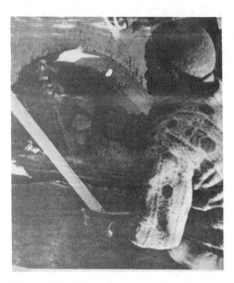

Photo 36   Trimming to precise diameter with the scraper.

Photo 37   The first plaster coat, note the lip. Photo shows the re-rod hanging suspended from the lip. The dirt walls are moistened before cement is applied.

Photo 39   Checking the walls for plumb before smoothing out the surface.

Photo 38   Placing the re-rod. Horizontals are in place and marks for vertical re-rod spacing are being made at equal intervals.

24 hours to allow the mortar time to cure. The second and subsequent lifts are carried out in the same way until water is reached, but make sure that the vertical re-rods are hooked and tied together with a 20cm overlap.

This method of making the lining is laborious as the plastering takes a lot of work, it often falls off the wall before it has set, and there is nothing to support the well until the mortar is completely set. Difficult, collapsing ground cannot be effectively tackled using this method.

Casting caisson rings without a mould

Undoubtedly the best method of casting caisson rings is to use a collapsible mould as described in Part II. When only one or two rings are required the following, more laborious method may be preferred since no mould is necessary.

A circular hole with the same diameter as that needed for the outer face of the concrete rings, is excavated in solid ground, and trimmed to the required depth using the methods described in Part II. The excavation is lined with reinforced mortar to a thickness of 10cm as described above under 'well lining without shutters'. Seepage holes are pricked through the mortar, and the ring is allowed to cure in the ground under cover.

After a week the ring is carefully dug out and taken away to cure under wet sacking until it is needed. These rings will not have the connecting bolts described in Part II, and if they are to be sunk through difficult ground, they should be cramped together during sinking using a wire rope and turn buckles, or threaded rod. Alternatively bolting lugs can be cast into the rings as they are made:—

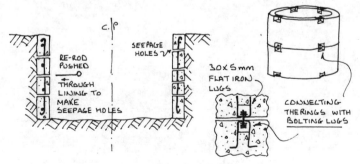

Making the caisson ring without a mould.

Photo 40   The re-rod is closely spaced so the casting will withstand the force of moving and lowering it into place.

Photo 41   Complete casting which has been watered. The small holes allow water flow into the well.

Photo 42   Digging up the casting.

Photo 43   Fixing casting into place by attaching to previous casting.

They are lowered into the well using ropes tied securely around the rings.

b) *Clay brick and masonry steining*

Before reinforced concrete came into general use as well lining material the normal method of building a shaft was to excavate and line with brickwork or masonry blocks. These materials can be used in caissoning (as will be described in the next chapter), but not in great depths or through unstable ground where collapsing earth walls prevent the lining from sinking. Brickwork and masonry are very weak under tension, and the stresses set up by collapsing earth sides can often fracture the linings, especially if this occurs on one side of the shaft only.

To avoid this hazard sink-and-line methods are commonly used, excavation proceeding in lifts restricted in length according to the unsupported strength of the excavated soil. The difficulty with this procedure is to support the completed lining of one lift while the one below is being excavated and lined, and this is overcome by a traditional method known as 'steining'. This is described below since it is still used in some parts of the world as an alternative to the more convenient methods described in Part II.

The well is dug in the usual way as deep as possible into

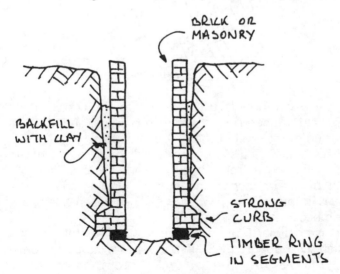

Build up lining on timber ring.

the ground until the walls become unstable. A ring made of timber segments the exact width of the lining is put together at the bottom of the well, and the lining built up to the surface. A curb is constructed just above the timber ring, and built to be part of the lining.

A narrow pit is excavated 2 metres or so into the centre of the well, blocks of wood are put into place, and strong timber props wedged solid on the blocks and under the timber ring:—

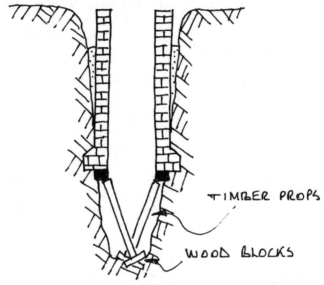

TIMBER PROPS

WOOD BLOCKS

Excavate below first lift.

The excavation is trimmed out to the correct diameter, a second timber ring is fitted into place, and the lining is built up to the level of the first lining lift.

The timber ring is now removed in segments, to prevent the lining above from collapsing, and the gaps solidly filled with bricks or stones and mortar. Digging and lining continues in this way until water is reached, when caisson sinking again becomes necessary.

It is possible to build the curb out of reinforced concrete, which will support the lining above as excavation continues. This removes the need for timber props, which are clumsy and make excavation and lining very difficult.

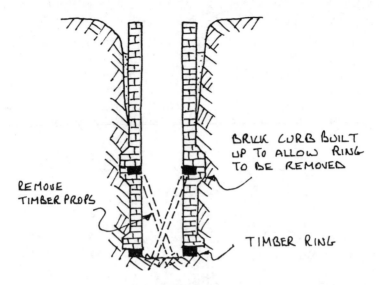

REMOVE
TIMBER PROPS

BRICK CURB BUILT
UP TO ALLOW RING
TO BE REMOVED

TIMBER RING

Building the second lift.

These reinforced concrete curbs must be cast in place, behind shutters made from either timber or a temporary brick walling, and given at least one week to cure. Their main advantage is that they use the minimum of concrete.

Brick and masonry are difficult to make watertight to prevent polluted surface water from soaking into the well. The space between the lining and the excavation for the top 3 metres must therefore be filled with puddled clay or cement mortar; the inside of the well above the water table should also be plastered to prevent the growth of vegetation and insect life:

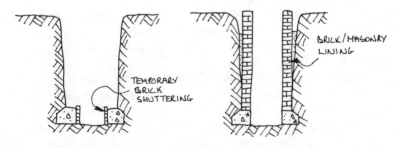

TEMPORARY
BRICK
SHUTTERING

BRICK/MASONRY
LINING

Cast concrete curb.   *Build brick lining on concrete curb.*

Caisson sinking using timber plank piling

Before reinforced concrete was developed less than a century ago, caisson linings were sunk using a timber cutting ring. An alternative method of caisson sinking employing timber plank piling is used in aquifers made up of loose, running sands.

The 2 metre long wooden planks are assembled at the bottom of the well to form the walls of a cylinder around two fabricated timber rings:—

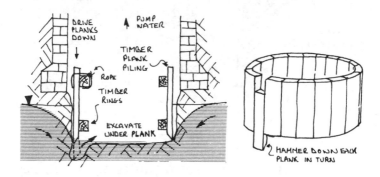

Timber caisson sinking.

Soil is dug out from under each plank in turn, each plank being sledge hammered downwards into the aquifer. The planks are tied to the top timber rings by ropes, which are loosened as the planks are driven down.

The planks are hammered in turn to a convenient depth and when they are at the same level, they are re-fastened to the top ring. The well is now excavated to the cutting edges of the planks, and the bottom ring pushed down to support the planks.

Sinking continues in this way until the tops of the planks are just above water level; a second caisson of timber planks is then sunk inside the first set, if necessary, to deepen the well, but you will only be able to do this to the extent that you can keep the water level down by baling or pumping.

The cutting edges of the planks are driven into the bottom of the well to prevent them from moving when the bottom ring is removed. The bottom ring is taken out and brick or masonry wall built up on the inside of the cylinder. The planks are unfastened from the top timber ring and pulled or

Photo 44   Brick Lined Well — India.

Photo 45   Masonry Lined Well — Upper Volta.

levered out of the aquifer in turn. The sand from the aquifer will collapse against the brick or masonry wall and be held in place.

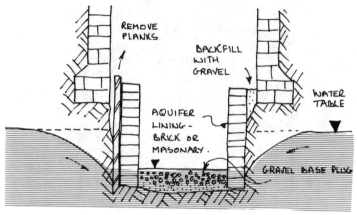

Constructing permanent aquifer lining.

This technique is also of great value when you expect to meet large cobbles or boulders in the aquifer. These will often throw the concrete block or pre-cast concrete ring caissons out of line. The heavy concrete caissons rest on the boulders which have to be dug out whilst under a great load from the caisson. The advantage of the timber piling is that each boulder can be picked out in turn before the planks are sunk onto them.

c)   Alternative materials for well lining

Timber cribbing

Where it is in cheap and plentiful supply, timber and bamboo have some use in well construction. They make only a temporary lining, however, and must be expected to rot and taint the water. You will often find that the effort and cost of digging and lining the well with timber is lost within a few years because of the timber collapsing or the well becoming grossly polluted. They should not be used to line wells used for drinking water unless no other materials are available.

However, timber and bamboo may be used successfully as a temporary cribbing around collapsing wells or for irrigation and cattle watering wells. Where timber and bamboo are in plentiful local supply they should not be overlooked for these types of well; treating the timber with a suitable preservative will lengthen its life by many years, but may taint the water for some time.

There are many methods of constructing the timber cribbing, but all of them have solid, bolted or rope bound horizontal timber frames of logs or square sawn timber with plank walls holding back the collapsing soils.

The well is excavated in a square section and sunk until the walls begin to collapse. A timber frame is built at the bottom of the well in the way shown below. The excavation is certain to be larger than the timber frame, and timber blocks or stones must be built up to wedge the frame. Planking is pushed behind the frame and tied, bolted or spiked into place. The second frame is built on top of the first, one or two metres up the well, depending on ground conditions, in exactly the same way, framing and planking continues until the surface is reached.

Pegs are driven into the walls under the frames to support the cribbing, and excavation and cribbing continues below in short lifts in the same way down to the water level. Caisson sinking will then be necessary.

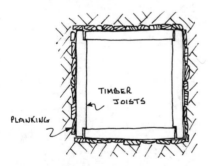

Timber cribbing supporting walls of well.

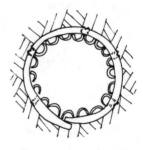

Split bamboo wrapped inside well, with vertical supports.

Steel and other pre-formed materials

Cast iron segments have been used widely in the past as the lining for mine shafts but their high cost makes it an unlikely material for water wells. Circular, corrugated, galvanised iron sections have also been used for linings but experience has

137

shown that this material corrodes within a few years and cannot stand up to shifting ground.

Plastics and glass fibre linings are new materials that are being tried but they would appear to be too expensive for most hand dug wells.

The main problem with these materials is to obtain a close intimate fit with the walls of the excavated well which will allow the stresses to be distributed as the ground moves. Their main advantages, with the exception of cast iron, are their relatively light weight which reduces considerably the costs of transportation to remote areas.

CHAPTER 15   ALTERNATIVE MATERIALS AND METHODS FOR CAISSONING FROM THE SURFACE

Caissoning, the method recommended for constructing the intake and that part of the shaft within the aquifer can be (and in many places is) used for the whole shaft from ground level downward. It is particularly useful for shallow wells and for those of larger than normal diameter such as those sunk into the banks of lakes or rivers where the surface water is liable to pollution but where there is a reservoir of naturally filtered water in the adjacent ground.

Under such circumstances caissoning has a number of advantages. The equipment used is simpler; a headframe is not essential; the amount of steel re-rod required for reinforced concrete is reduced; practically the whole of the construction work is carried out on the surface; advance site preparation and prefabrication techniques can speed up work considerably.

There are disadvantages and these multiply with the depth of the well. It is difficult to keep the shaft vertical; boulders or even large stones in the ground can cause the caisson to tilt, because there are no curbs, the stability of the lining depends entirely upon skin friction; since this friction between lining and shaft wall is irregular, stresses are set up which may cause slipping, jamming or opening of construction joints. As the depth increases the tendency for sections to 'hang' (causing tension failure), or to buckle or crush under the weight of the caisson tube, becomes greater. It is also possible to contaminate the aquifer by seepage from the surface down the outside of the caisson.

For these reasons caisson wells are popular where the depth is shallow and the ground free from boulders or other obstructions. As a general rule the method is not recommended where the total depth is more than 8 or 10 times the internal diameter, though it is only fair to point out that this limitation has often been successfully exceeded, especially in India, by teams with long experience of this type of construction. The following notes refer to caisson wells of 10 metres or less in depth with a finished diameter of between 1 and 2 metres. For large diameter caissons special construction techniques are necessary, which involve engineering skills outside the scope of this manual.

Materials for caisson lining

The materials most commonly used for caissons are reinforced concrete rings, clay or concrete bricks and masonry. The construction technique will depend upon the material to be used, the biggest difference being between prefabricated concrete rings on the one hand and walling materials built up on site on the other. Concrete rings, which have to be bolted or otherwise fastened together to form a continuous tube, require no special foundation during sinking and, because they have been cast well in advance and have been 'cured', are strong enough to withstand external loads immediately they are put in place. Masonry blocks or fired clay brickwork have to pass through a period of great weakness immediately after laying and until the cement mortar bonding has set and hardened. Even then the linings of these materials are weak in tension. Consequently it is necessary first to build a foundation (known as a cutting ring) upon which the lining will be built. This foundation is nearly always of reinforced concrete (though sometimes timber is used) and it must be heavy and strong enough to resist pressures that might otherwise distort and rupture the lining above.

Caisson sinking using pre-cast concrete rings

In Chapter 9 a description was given of how to pre-cast concrete caisson rings. The same technique is used when caissoning from the surface, and the method described is probably the simplest and most satisfactory, both as regards the rings themselves and their assembly into a continuous tube.

The ring sections are heavy — about 700kg for 1 metre, 350kg for 0.5 metre — and although keeping to the smaller height takes longer to fabricate and requires twice the number of joints there is the compensating advantage that lighter lifting tackle is necessary. For caissoning this will usually consist of a tripod of shear legs with pulley over the mouth of the shaft, the lifting rope being controlled by a brake post as described in Chapter 14.

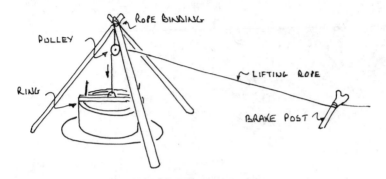

Lowering pre-cast concrete rings by a tripod.

To keep lifting to a minimum an excavation is made to a depth of two or three rings, the floor levelled, the rings rolled to the side of the well and lowered (using the stretcher and spacers described in Chapter 9). From then on the rings will be added one at a time as the caisson tube descends during excavation. Thus no ring need be lifted more than half its own height.

Pre-cast R.C. rings are widely used to make road culverts, manholes, sewers, etc., and if these are available in your area, they can be adapted for caisson sinking. The main difficulty with these rings is that they cannot be bolted together, and in unstable soils, you may find them impossible to use, as they will jam and tilt out of line.

One solution to this is to strap the column together using wire rope, hooks, and small hand winches.

The rings are lowered into the excavation, mortared together, then compressed using hand winches, (which are often employed to pull out tree stumps). The ropes are loosened and unhooked at the surface after the column of rings has settled, to allow extra rings to be added on top. They are attached again and re-tensioned before sinking begins again.

Photo 46   Pre-cast Reinforce Concrete Rings for Caisson Sinking — a) Concrete rings ar heavy to manhandle around the site.

Photo 47   b) Lowering the rings into the well is difficult unless the headframe and winding gear are strong.

Photo 48   c) Caisson sinkin shallow well on the bank of river will give a clean and plentiful supply of water.

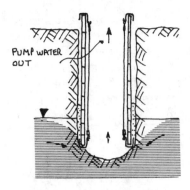

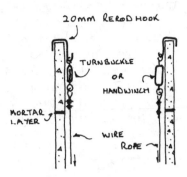

Dig down to aquifer. Then build caisson to surface.

Strapping the rings together.

A further difficulty with the commercial pre-cast R.C. rings is that they are impermeable, and water will only be able to enter the well from the bottom. You should therefore consider making special permeable rings to allow the ground water to flow freely into the well.

Finishing and maintaining the well has already been described in Part II. A porous concrete plug is usually placed at the bottom of the well, or a gravel layer, to help prevent silt and sand from being drawn up into the well if it is over pumped. Puddled clay should be back filled into the top 3 metres behind the caisson; if concrete is back filled to seal the aquifer from contamination, there is the possiblity that subsequent settling of the well will cause the joints between the rings to open up, because the concrete will bond with the top rings and prevent them from settling. The wire ropes can, if necessary, be replaced by hooked re-rod, cut and welded to the correct length.

Caisson sinking using a timber cutting ring

The use of a cutting ring is best illustrated by a brief description of a form of well construction, very prevalent for shallow domestic wells in Europe until a century or so ago. This used a wooden cutting ring upon which a brick lining was built up.

The well was first excavated down to the water table and as far below as safety would permit. A timber ring was fabricated on the surface, dismantled, and reassembled at the

143

bottom of the excavation. Brickwork was built on this ring up to the surface. Time was given for the mortar to set thoroughly, after which excavation was carried out inside the ring causing the whole tube of brickwork to descend. As the top dropped below ground level additional brick courses were added until the lining reached its final position, which was usually when the water inside the brickwork became too deep for excavation to continue.

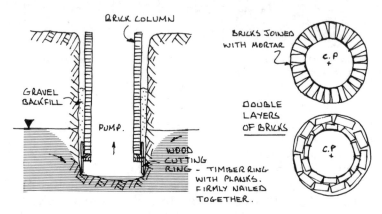

Brick caisson lining.

It is possible to adopt this method today, virtually unchanged, especially for wells used for purposes other than providing drinking water. Indeed for shallow wells it is probably the cheapest of all techniques, requiring no head-gear, no shutters or moulds. The principal disadvantage is that the wood cutting ring will rot in due course, and this may lead to the collapse of the brick lining.

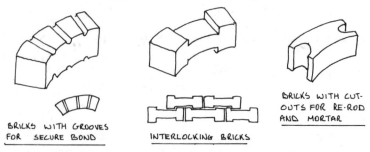

Special bricks for brick lining.

144

Various adaptations of this method involve the use of special bricks that are easier, quicker and stronger to lay, or that can be made to incorporate vertical re-rods to add strength to the lining.

When the brickwork reaches the surface a brick and mortar or concrete slab is laid around the lining with a clearance all round of about 5cm. This slab, which is later incorporated into the drainage apron, helps to keep the additional brickwork courses truly level and circular, and the 5cm gap allows gravel to be fed down outside the brickwork.

It should be noted that it is virtually impossible to prevent contamination seeping down outside the brickwork and polluting the intake and aquifer. Using concrete instead of gravel outside the brickwork may reduce, but will not prevent, such percolation and will add to the risk of cracking the brickwork if any movement of the ground takes place.

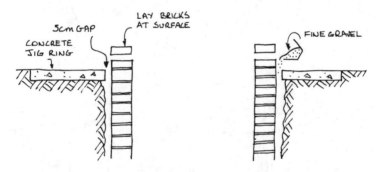

Concrete ring guiding laying and sinking of brick column.

The inside of the well, above the water table, should be plastered and trowelled with a 1:4 mix of cement and sand mortar to prevent moss and insects from establishing themselves in the joints between the bricks.

Reinforced concrete cutting rings for brick, masonry or concrete block caissons

Today reinforced concrete has almost entirely superseded timber as material for making cutting rings. Concrete rings are usually cast below ground at the bottom of an excavation a few metres deep, corresponding roughly to the first lift of

145

a well built by sink-and-line techniques. To cast a ring special shutters are used, which are assembled on the surface and lowered into position. They may be made from sheet metal or of plywood, but must be so designed that they can be dismantled once the ring has been cast in position.

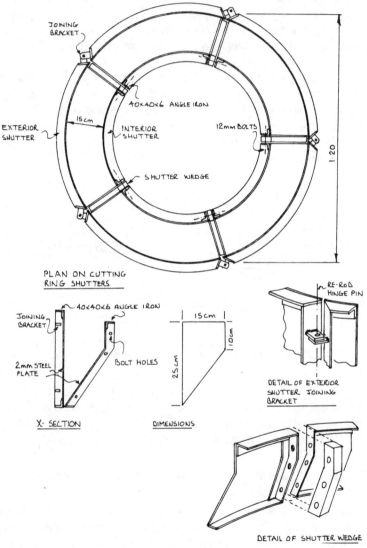

PLAN ON CUTTING RING SHUTTERS

X-SECTION

DIMENSIONS

DETAIL OF EXTERIOR SHUTTER JOINING BRACKET

DETAIL OF SHUTTER WEDGE

Cutting ring mould.

The re-rod reinforcing cage for the cutting ring is built on the surface and requires careful supervision. The vertical trapezoidal frames for the cutting ring are formed by bending them around a wooden jig; these will provide the starter bars for the caisson re-rod cage, and must be strong enough to take the loads. It is usual to make the frames from 5mm re-rod, as this diameter can be bent by hand, although thicker re-rod can be used. Forty-eight frames are made from the 5mm re-rod and bundled and tied together to give sixteen sets of three.

The horizontal rings are made from 8mm re-rod, two rings at 112cm diameter, and one ring at 100cm diameter; it is easiest to make and tie the rings on the ground around circles marked and pegged out in the same manner already described for the horizontal re-rod of the main lining. The rings should be given a 20cm overlap, and be tightly tied together.

The trapezoidal frames are threaded over the rings, and distributed in sets of three around the cage. Use one of the concrete blocks to make sure that the frames are in the correct position to provide starter bars for the vertical caisson re-rod:—

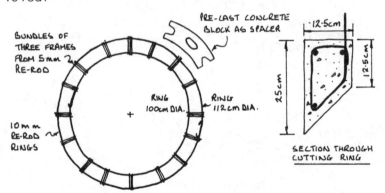

Making the cutting ring re-rod cage.

Assembling the cutting ring re-rod cage is a very tricky operation as the re-rod continually bends out of shape. You will find it much easier to make if you lift the cage into the shutters before you tie the rods together. This holds the cage in the correct shape (see diagram on page 150).

147

Photo 49   Building Up The Cutting Ring Mould —
a) Assemble interior sections. — Upper Volta.

Photo: Simon Watt

Photo: Simon Watt

Photo 50
b) Assemble exterior sections. — Upper Volta.

Photo: Simon Watt

Photo 51
c) Tighten up bolts holding sections together. -- Upper Volta.

Photos. Simon Watt

Photo 52 Building Up The Cutting Ring Mould — d) Removeable wedges to loosen sections for removal. — Upper Volta.

Photo 53 e) Exterior sections are held together with re-rod. The re-rod is pulled out to allow them to be dismantled and removed. — Upper Volta.

Photo 54 f) Lower assembled sections into well. — Upper Volta.

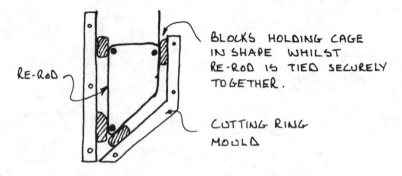

RE-ROD

BLOCKS HOLDING CAGE IN SHAPE WHILST RE-ROD IS TIED SECURELY TOGETHER.

CUTTING RING MOULD

Holding the cutting ring whilst tying.

When you are ready to make the cutting ring, lower the oiled and assembled set of shutters into the well. Carefully check that they are blocked up both level and central, because this will determine the correct line of the caisson. Lower the re-rod frame, and place it into the shutters using small stones to keep the frame away from the faces. Check again that the shutters are level and fill them with a 1:2:4 mix (cement:sand:gravel) of concrete, evenly all round. Tamp the wet concrete to compact the mix and remove air bubbles and then skim the top level. The top should be left slightly rough to help the bond with the first layer of blocks. Check carefully that the re-rods sticking up out of the ring are in the correct position for the blocks. When the concrete has set slightly, trowel out holes around the starter bars to allow them to be cranked later into the correct position:—

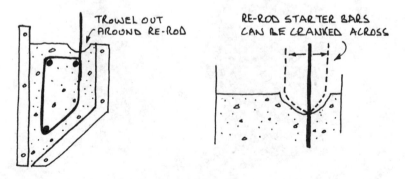

TROWEL OUT AROUND RE-ROD

RE-ROD STARTER BARS CAN BE CRANKED ACROSS

Cranking starter bars.

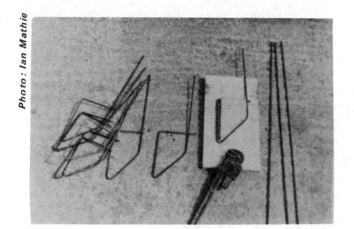

Photo 55   *Preparing the Cutting Ring Ready for the Pre-cast Blocks — a) Bend re-rod around wooden jig.*

Photo 56   *b) Loosely assemble re-rod frame ready for placement in cutting ring mould. In the photograph 10mm re-rod was used. Notice the starter bars from trapezoidal frames.*

Photo 57   Preparing the Cutting Ring Ready for the Pr[e]cast Blocks — c) When cutting ring has cured, remove mould sections by excavating below ring.

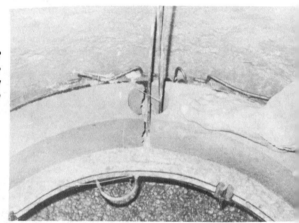

Photo 58 d) Place a complete circle of the concrete blocks on the cutting ring to check the position of the starter bars.

Photo 59 e) If starter bars are in the wrong position, crank them across.

It is possible, though not so satisfactory, to cast the cutting ring on the surface without using shutters, and then lower this into position. The ring is heavy, can become stuck fast as it is being lowered and the cutting edge can be damaged, but it saves the cost of shutters. These shutters are an expensive item as they are difficult to fabricate.

The cutting ring mould is built into the ground by the method shown in Photos 60-66. The reinforcing cage is constructed and fixed in the mould and the concrete mix is poured and tamped. The re-rod is cut and fixed in a similar way to that just described for use in a set of shutters.

Building up a caisson on a concrete cutting ring

The following description of building a caisson of concrete blocks on a reinforced concrete cutting ring is equally applicable to the construction of a well totally caissoned from the surface, or to an alternative method of caissoning for telescoping within a lined shaft. To avoid repetition the latter is described, and should be read in conjunction with Chapter 9.

It should also be noted that the method may be applied to linings built of masonry or brickwork on cutting rings.

The caisson is built up several metres high on the cutting ring at the base of the main lining tube and the mortar between the blocks is given at least a week to set before excavation begins. The concrete blocks for the caisson, and the re-rod cage for the cutting ring, should already have been made up on the surface during the construction of the main section of the well. The necessity of allowing a week for the mortar to set is a major limitation of this method.

Making the pre-cast concrete, caisson blocks

The concrete blocks are made in special oiled moulds using a fairly dry concrete mix of 1:2.5:5 (cement:sand:gravel). The concrete is vibrated to compaction by tapping the sides of the mould with blocks of wood — the surface of the mould is then trowelled smooth. After ten minutes or so, the mould is lifted up leaving the green concrete brick on the ground: the mould is then cleaned, oiled, and ready for the next casting. The blocks are allowed to set for twenty four hours under wet sacking or plastic sheets before they are moved to

Photo 60 Making the Cutting Ring Without a Mould
a) Mark out ring on ground and dig roughly to size.

Photo 61
b) Line the mould with a weak 1:15 (cement:sand) mortar and obtain correct shape using jig and radius arm.

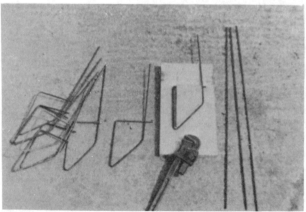

Photo 62
c) Cut and bend re-rod to shape

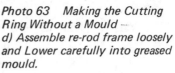

Photo 63   Making the Cutting
Ring Without a Mould —
d) Assemble re-rod frame loosely
and Lower carefully into greased
mould.

Photo 64
e) Wedge frame to shape using pebbles, then tie
frame securely. (right)

Photo 65
f) Fill mould with concrete and tamp to consolidate
and remove air bubbles. (left)

Photo 66
g) Leave ring one week to cure
then dig out and clean.

a shady place for curing, again under wet sacking or grass. They must be kept damp or they will dry out and become cracked. It is most important that the blocks have good sharp edges, as this helps you to lay them accurately.

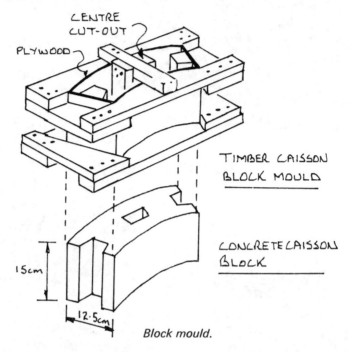

Block mould.

The blocks are quick to lay, because they can be fitted over the vertical re-rods; they can also be lifted off, or placed on one side of the caisson, if the caisson begins to tilt during sinking.

Building the caisson lining

The caisson ring must be given at least 3 days to cure. When it is ready the shutters are stripped away, and extra lengths of 8mm diameter re-rod 1.5m long are tied to the starter bars. A layer of sand:cement mortar is trowelled onto the ring top and a circle of blocks is laid. If the re-rod starter bars are out of position, crank them across using a hammer or wrench.

The blocks are built 4 layers deep at a time with no mortar between the layers. At the fifth layer, mortar is trowelled onto the blocks; it is also tamped carefully into the holes in the blocks around the vertical re-rod. A horizontal circle of re-rod is placed and tied on the outside of the vertical re-rod, covered with another layer of mortar and another lift of blocks built on top. The thin cracks between the blocks allow water to seep slowly into the well whilst holding back the sand. The caisson becomes in effect a cage of reinforced concrete, in-filled with blocks.

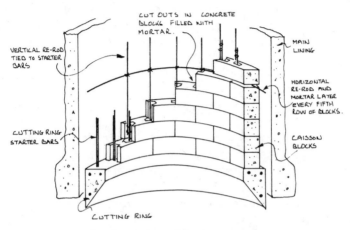

Sectional view of aquifer caisson.

The caisson is built one and a half metres high inside the main lining, which provides a guide for the caisson and helps prevent it from falling out of line during sinking. Additional lengths of 8mm diameter vertical re-rod are then tied to the first set of re-rods, a temporary plank platform is laid across the top of the caisson, and the caisson is built another 1.5m higher. The caisson will now be 3m high, and excavation can begin as soon as the mortar has been given time to set, at least 7 days.

The directions given in Chapter 9 may now be followed to the completion of the well.

Porous concrete blocks for caisson sinking

The solid concrete caisson blocks described above allow water to enter the well through the seepage cracks between the unmortared blocks. These blocks can also be made using porous concrete; these blocks can be used in collapsing silty aquifers to increase the seepage area of the caisson.

The mould is carefully built and oiled ready for use. Porous, light weight concrete is made from a mix of 1:1:4 (cement:sand:gravel) using gravel that passes a 10mm sieve but stays on a 5mm sieve. The sand and gravel are first thoroughly wetted and the cement is added with extra water if necessary and mixed into the aggregate. The dry mix is then poured into the mould and vibrated to compaction. After 15 minutes or so, carefully lift off the mould and clean and oil the inside ready for the next block. The blocks must be cured for at least a week under damp sacking, as light weight concrete fractures very easily.

The porous blocks are built up on the cutting ring using a layer of mortar on the edge of each block. A horizontal re-rod ring is built in at every course of blocks. This method of making the blocks for the caisson ring should only be used in very fine sand or silt aquifers where the seepage cracks of the solid blocks may be too wide and allow the fine sands to wash into the well, resulting in caving and collapse. The corners and edges of the blocks will be rough, and will always need to be mortared together. They are more difficult to use than solid blocks.

In situ reinforced concrete rings

Another alternative method of caissoning is to pour concrete into a special mould which has been lowered into the well and assembled on the already prepared cutting ring around the re-rod cage. Concrete is poured into the mould — seepage holes are built into the casting using removable rods which are pulled out of the casting when it has set. The mould is stripped after a few days and additional rings cast on top. In practice, it is often found that the caisson tube tilts during casting, trapping the external mould shutter; the caisson has then to be straightened up by excavating under the caisson and jacking the caisson vertical. This is both difficult and time consuming. Filling the space between the caisson lining and the permanent lining with small round gravel helps to hold the caisson upright.

This method, which is favoured by some well diggers, is not recommended, as besides the difficulties which can arise when the caisson tube tilts the caisson must be given several weeks to cure before it is sunk.

Photo 67   Using Porous Concrete Blocks for Caisson Sinking — a) Make the blocks in the mould. This mould is 20cm deep.

Photos: Simon Watt

Photo 68
b) Mix the concrete to a dry consistency, pour it into the mould and compact it by banging mould sides with wood blocks. Leave for 15 minutes before lifting mould.

Photo 69
c) Cure blocks under wet sacking for seven days. Check that they are porous by pouring water on them. If they are impermeable, change mix with less sand.

Photo 70
d) Check cutting ring starter bars and crank them into place if necessary. Attach vertical re-rod, trowel mortar onto ring and fit blocks over re-rod. (Caisson built above ground for demonstration purpose).

*Photo 71   Using Porous Concrete Blocks
for Caisson Sinking — e) Trowel mortar
into gaps between blocks and fill cut-
outs around re-rod with mortar.*

*Photo 72   f) On every course of blocks a horizontal re-rod
is tied, laid on a bed of mortar and the next row of blocks
laid.*

CHAPTER 16   IMPROVING EXISTING WELLS

When a new sanitary well has been completed and put into use, replacing an old, insanitary, unprotected one, there are two courses open to the builder. Either the old well must be made sanitary and allowed to be used in conjunction with the new one, or it must be filled in and made unusable. Under no circumstances should it just be left in a dangerous and insanitary state or used as a refuse tip.

Rehabilitation of an old well may precede the construction of a new one; temporary improvements may cost little and be carried out quickly, and they may remove health hazards to consumers even while the new well is being constructed.

Sometimes there are social, sentimental or historical reasons why villagers insist on continuing to use an old well in preference to a new one. Instead of attempting to overcome local prejudices it may be preferable to try and improve the standard of the old and not endeavour to force acceptance of the new.

The simplest, but most important, single improvement to an existing well is the construction of a wellhead consisting of headwall and drainage apron. This single measure can eradicate guinea worm and considerably reduce other health risks. It can only be done on its own in good solid ground where there is no danger of the shaft collapsing; if the ground is at all unstable some form of lining must be inserted.

Dealing first with an unlined well with a reasonably small mouth to the top of the shaft the initial task is to clear all rubbish and loose silt from the bottom. For this purpose obviously a sinker has to descend on a ladder or rope (according to the depth involved) and he should take note of the condition of the shaft wall, in particular whether there is any dangerous overhang.

The ground around the well top is graded to ensure that rainwater and spillage drains away from the shaft, after which a headwall and drainage apron are constructed in permanent material:—

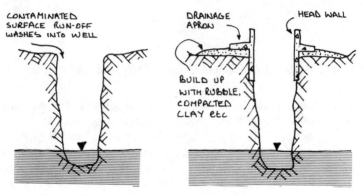

Improving an existing open well by constructing a concrete wellhead.

Reinforced concrete is usually the simplest and cheapest material for this purpose, and temporary shuttering may be made from old oil drums or timber. Brickwork, masonry, even cement mortar may be used instead of concrete.

If there is the slightest doubt about the stability of the shaft, or if the well is one that receives a great deal of use, it is always desirable to install a lining. Caissoning (as described in the preceding chapter) is probably the simplest method in an old excavation, the lining being built up on a concrete cutting ring. Another advantage is that the well can be deepened at the same time should this be required. Because

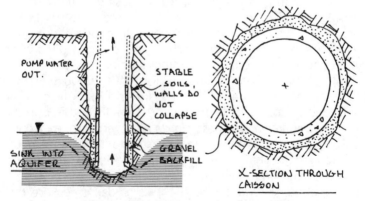

Backfill behind caisson with small gravel.

Photo: Simon Watt

Photo 73 Improving The Wellhead — a) The wellhead has been built up with masonry to provide a drainage apron, a thin lip wall has been made from concrete to prevent spilt water running back into the well. — Upper Volta.

Photo: Simon Watt

Photo 74 b) Headwall made from plastered concrete blocks. The well is constructed in solid ground and is unlined. The headwall prevents polluted run-off from entering the well. — Upper Volta.

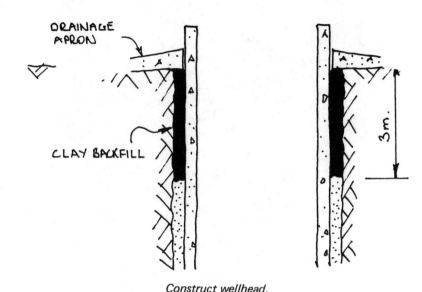

Construct wellhead.

the old excavation will almost certainly be irregular in shape there is likely to be a considerable gap between the caisson (which should be circular) and parts of the shaft wall. This space should be filled with gravel, except for the top 3 metres which should be plugged with puddled clay before the wellhead is constructed.

Sealed wells

One method of improving an existing dangerous or insanitary well is to convert it to what is known as a 'sealed' well — one in which the only access to the intake is through a small diameter pipe leading to the surface. In some ways this is cheaper than rehabilitating the well in the conventional manner; it is not necessary to line the shaft, for example. On the other hand this method calls for the installation (and therefore for the continued maintenance) of a hand pump, which may outweigh the financial saving, and should the pump break down there is no alternative way of extracting the water. Once sealed it is not possible to deepen the well, or to extract any sand that may have entered with the water.

Despite these disadvantages the speed and cheapness of the method have made it popular in various countries (with relatively minor variations). The following description is of one type used very successfully in parts of India.

It consists of a caisson lining sunk into the aquifer, closed on top by a reinforced concrete slab, and with a narrow concrete tube built up to the surface to take a pump rising main. The well is back filled with soil around the concrete tube and the wellhead built up 0.5m above ground level.

The caisson is built inside the existing well, using either a cutting ring and concrete blocks, baked clay bricks or more usually, pre-cast reinforced concrete rings as described in Chapter 15. The sides of the well may need a temporary crib for support if they show signs of collapse.

The caisson is sunk as deep as possible into the aquifer. You should carry out the sinking in the dry season when the water level has fallen to its lowest level, because once the well is sealed, you will not be able to deepen it. The space between the caisson and the well sides is filled with clean sand, and a base plug built at the well bottom; the sand around the caisson will also act as a reservoir to store water.

A reinforced concrete slab with a hole in the centre is cast on the surface and when it has cured for at least 7 days it is lowered into the well and mortared in place on top of the caisson rings. The slab may be cast in a mould formed by digging out a shallow hole in the ground to the correct size, lining this with plastic sheeting, fixing the reinforcement and pouring the concrete; the slab must have four lifting hooks to attach the lowering ropes. The reinforcement in the concrete must be at the bottom of the slab when it is placed in the well, to strengthen the concrete against the weight of the back fill.

Small diameter concrete pipes are now built up on the slab, and the slab covered with a thick layer of sand to filter water percolating down from the surface. Back filling with earth or clay continues against the concrete pipes until the hole is completely filled to the surface, with the pipes rising about 0.5m above ground level. The soil used as back filling must be added in layers, dampened with water and thoroughly compacted, otherwise it will settle and cause the wellhead apron to fracture.

The narrow pipe rising to the surface can be made of any material and it must be sealed to prevent polluted surface water from soaking in. The joints between the pipes are usually mortared solid. Clay pipes, bricks and plastic piping have all been used, but the pipe must be strong enough to stand up to the soil pressure, be durable, and large enough to take the rising main pipe for the hand pump.

Mound up the back fill on the surface around the pipe, build the apron and drainage ditch, disinfect the well and fix the hand pump — the well will now be ready for use.

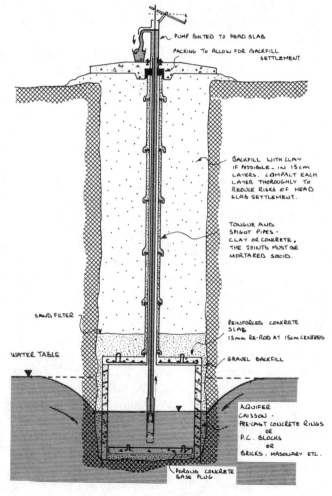

Section through shallow sealed well.

CHAPTER 17   IMPROVING THE YIELD OF A WELL

There are two principal ways in which the amount of water entering a well may be increased — by deepening it, thus producing a greater difference of water level between the inside and outside of the intake, and by increasing the area of the intake in contact with the aquifer. There is a third way — by making the intake lining more porous — but this is often self-defeating since sand or other aquifer material is likely to enter and choke the well.

Deepening a well is usually (not always but usually) the most satisfactory way of increasing its yield. However, the limiting factor controlling the degree to which deepening can be carried out in practice is the difficulty of keeping the water level inside the shaft sufficiently low for the sinkers to continue working. Unless clearing pumps are available (and these can cause caving and collapse if they are not carefully controlled) the level has to be kept down by baling, and even under good conditions this limits the penetration of the aquifer to a maximum of about 3 metres. As has been explained earlier the only satisfactory technique in the majority of cases is to leave the well unfinished until the end of the dry season and deepen it then.

To increase the infiltration area of the intake the most obvious method is to make its diameter larger, but this is virtually impossible in an existing well and often inconvenient and expensive in a new construction.

The infiltration area, or effective diameter of the well can be enlarged by driving tunnels or pipes into the sides of the well below the water table. This allows ground water from a wide radius to flow more easily into the well.

The well may also be deepened by driving or boring a well point into the bottom; a small diameter pump must then be used to extract water unless the water flows up into the well from a deeper aquifer under artesian pressure.

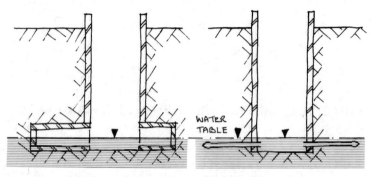

Tunnels or adits constructed at bottom of well.

Porous pipes driven through well lining.

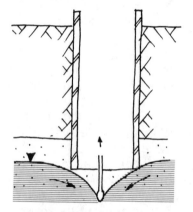

Porous pipe driven or bored into base of well.

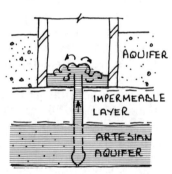

Penetrating down to an artesian aquifer.

Tunnels or adits are driven by hand and can be less than 1 metre high by 0.5 metre wide. They should be level or sloping upward from the well shaft, and be lined with bricks or concrete sections as digging proceeds. Well lining shutters can be used as form work and temporary linings to larger diameter hand excavated horizontal galleries.

A 0.5 metre deep section of adit is excavated through the side of the well. It is lined at the lower half by bricks or reinforced concrete, and taken up to the centre line (Stages 1 and 2 in diagram). A section of 0.5 metre shutter is erected on the construction lining and bolted together (Stage 3). The lining is then built up over the shutter to form a ring, and the

168

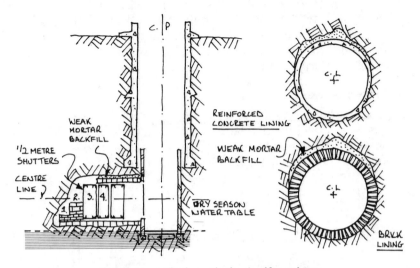

Driving an adit through the aquifer caisson.

over cutting in the top half of the excavation back filled with a weak mortar mixture. (Stage 4). The adit is driven in this way, with the shutters left in place to support the lining as it sets. Only 0.5 metre of excavation is left unsupported at any one time and the risk of collapse is therefore minimised.

Thrust tubes

Perforated galvanised steel pipes with points fitted can be thrust horizontally through the sides of a well using car jacks. This method is simpler and less costly than the driven adits;

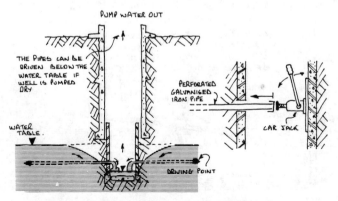

Perforated pipes driven through aquifer caisson.

the main advantage of the adits however, is their greater volume which allows far more water storage. Many pipes can be driven into the sides of the well; this can be done under water, or in the bottom of a pumped well.

Connected wells

In some shallow aquifers, wells are constructed close together in a line, and joined together with a tunnel or bored pipe. Only one of the wells is left open, the rest are covered over and back filled, giving a large saving in lining material.

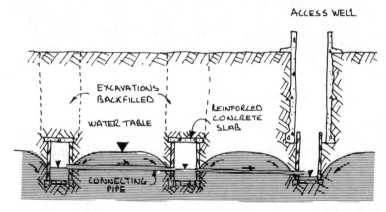

Connected wells.

A very old variation on this technique is the traditional Persian quanat, which used exploratory wells and a driven adit as a way of reaching ground water to avoid the need to

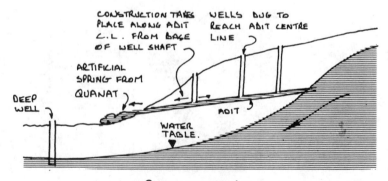

Quanat construction.

pump the water up from a well. The quanat is in effect an artificial spring — the adit may be several kilometres long.

This technique has been brought up to date by horizontal drilling, i.e. drilling a bore hole sideways into a hill to tap the aquifer.

PART IV A DESCRIPTION OF STANDARD EQUIPMENT AND MATERIALS

CHAPTER 18   SCHEDULE OF EQUIPMENT

The following is a schedule of the tools and equipment required to carry out a well sinking programme using the procedure described in Part II of this manual. The quantities given are those normally supplied to each well team; it is obviously possible to operate using less numbers of certain items, but experience has shown that the list represents a desirable standard below which inefficiency may occur or delays result.

Notes on the use of the various items and on possible alternatives are given in a later chapter to avoid possible confusion. For clarity the item numbers given in the schedule are the same as those used in Chapter 19 so that cross reference can be made. Specifications are given in the schedule to help in ordering those items that have to be purchased.

A. SPECIALLY MADE OR PURCHASED EQUIPMENT

1. **Headframe.** The type described and illustrated overleaf was developed in Northern Nigeria, where it is referred to as type 'G'. It is constructed with four legs of 65x65x6mm angle iron, crossed braced with 40 x 40 x 6mm iron. It is 4.5 metres high to the centre of the main headsheave, 4 metres between front and back legs, the front legs are 1.2 metres apart, and the back legs 2 metres apart. To the front legs at a convenient height is fixed the winding gear, with a 3:1 ratio cast iron gear, winding handles, hand brake and a simple arrangement whereby the hoisting drum (which can carry about 150m of 12mm diameter wire rope) can be freed from the gearing but not from the brake. An auxiliary headsheave for the concreting rope is fixed about 60cm from the top of the back legs. The whole can be dismantled and each piece is light enough to be carried by a man, so that it is transportable where there are no roads.

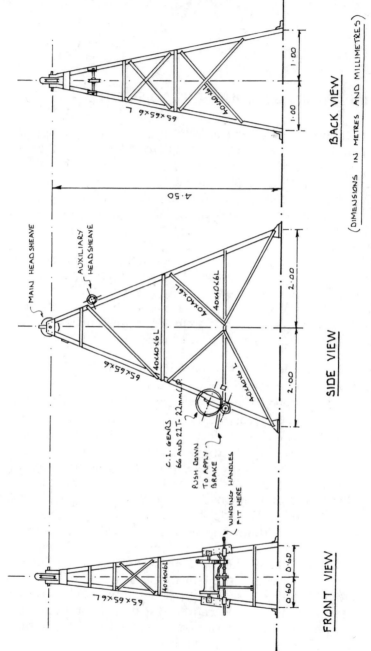

FRONT VIEW

SIDE VIEW

BACK VIEW

(DIMENSIONS IN METRES AND MILLIMETRES)

Item 1. Northern Nigeria type 'G' headframe.

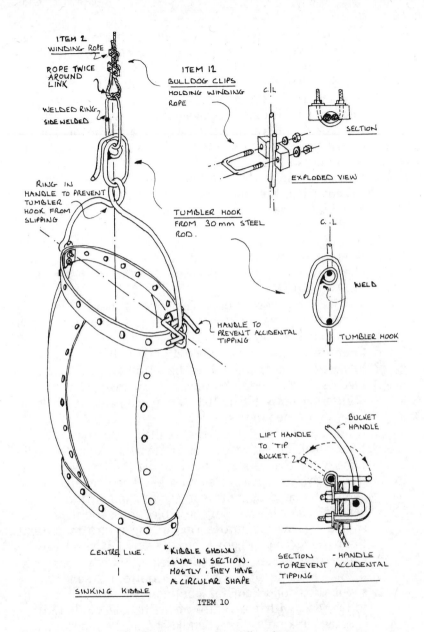

ITEM 2
WINDING ROPE

ROPE TWICE
AROUND
LINK

WELDED RING
SIDE WELDED

ITEM 12
BULLDOG CLIPS
HOLDING WINDING
ROPE

C.L.

SECTION

EXPLODED VIEW

RING IN
HANDLE TO PREVENT
TUMBLER
HOOK FROM
SLIPPING

TUMBLER HOOK
FROM 30 mm STEEL
ROD.

C.L.

WELD

HANDLE TO
PREVENT ACCIDENTAL
TIPPING

TUMBLER HOOK

BUCKET
HANDLE

LIFT HANDLE
TO 'TIP
BUCKET.

CENTRE LINE.

* KIBBLE SHOWN
OVAL IN SECTION.
MOSTLY, THEY HAVE
A CIRCULAR SHAPE

SINKING KIBBLE *

ITEM 10

SECTION – HANDLE
TO PREVENT ACCIDENTAL
TIPPING

Kibbles for removing soil and water.

Similar (and equally effective) headframes are in use in other countries but the one shown is known to have a reputation for simplicity and durability acquired after use over many years on some thousands of wells.

2. **Winding rope** (125m) 12mm diameter, ordinary lay steel wire, best flexible ungalvanised, tensile strength of material 15 metric tons per square centimetre, acid grade, actual breaking strain 7.3 metric tons, stranded 6 x 19 with fibre core.

3. **Concrete feed rope** (125m) 6mm diameter, best engineering guy rope, of similar specification to item 2.

4. **Plumbing rope** (125m) 3mm, best engineering guy rope, of similar specification to item 2.

5. **Shuttering** (six sets), each set consisting of 2mm thick steel plate sections welded to 50mm x 30mm rolled channel ribs to form together a 1.30m diameter circle 1 metre high.

   Note. The illustration which follows shows a set of 4 sections making the circle; sets of 3 (assembling to the same diameter) are equally suitable.

6. **Shuttering** (two sets) as item 5 but 0.5m high.

7. **Wedges** for shuttering (24 wedges) 1m long.

8. **Wedges** for shuttering (8 wedges) 0.5m long.

9. **Shuttering bolts** (96 bolts) 12mm diameter 10cm long, hexagon headed mild steel.

10. **Kibbles** sinking (2 kibbles) 60 litre capacity, made of thick steel, either welded or riveted but must be watertight, with the handle hinged at the top rim and not at the centre, so that it cannot tip up. The diameter at the centre should be greater than the top and bottom to prevent any risk of it catching on projections, and the handle should be twisted into a ring in the centre to prevent tipping sideways. Weight approximately 18kg each.

11. **Concreting buckets** (2 buckets) height of body 25cm, diameter at top 30cm, diameter of bottom 20cm. With a spout projecting 8cm for pouring concrete behind shuttering, and with the centre of the handle twisted into a ring as for kibbles. The handle should be hinged at the top rim of the bucket.

12. **Bulldog clips** (12 clips) for 12mm winding rope.

13. **Bulldog clips** (12 clips) for 6mm concrete feed rope.

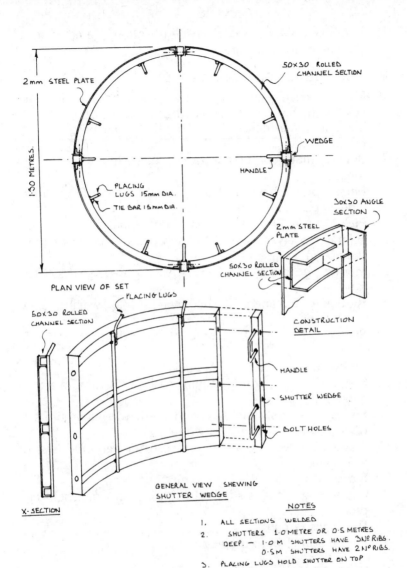

Plan view of set — *2mm steel plate, 1·30 metres, 50×30 rolled channel section, wedge, handle, placing lugs 15mm dia., tie bar 15mm dia.*

Construction detail — *50×30 angle section, 2mm steel plate, 50×30 rolled channel section*

General view shewing shutter wedge — *50×30 rolled channel section, placing lugs, handle, shutter wedge, bolt holes, X-section*

NOTES

1. ALL SECTIONS WELDED
2. SHUTTERS 1·0 METRE OR 0·5 METRES DEEP. — 1·0 M SHUTTERS HAVE 3 N° RIBS. 0·5 M SHUTTERS HAVE 2 N° RIBS.
3. PLACING LUGS HOLD SHUTTER ON TOP IN PLACE.

Concrete shutters 1.30 metres diameter.

14. **Bulldog clips** (12 clips) for 3mm plumbing rope.
15. **Thimbles** (6 thimbles) for 12mm winding rope.
16. **Thimbles** (6 thimbles) for 6mm concrete feed rope.
17. **Thimbles** (6 thimbles) for 3mm plumbing rope.

18. **Tumbler hooks** (1 hook) made of 20mm diameter steel, the link welded at the side.

B. SINKING AND CONCRETING TOOLS

19. **Miners bars** (2 bars) 1.5m long made from 3cm diameter steel with chisel at one end and point at the other.
20. **Trimming mattocks** (2 mattocks) 1.5 kg weight, shaft 60cm long.
21. **Sinking mattocks** (1 mattock) 2kg weight, shaft 60 cm long.
22. **Miners pick** (2 picks) 1.5 kg weight, shafts 60cm long. One end chisel, one end point.
23. **Pick** (1 pick) 2kg weight, shaft 90cm long.
24. **Filling shovels** (2 shovels) round nosed, shafts not more than 60cm long.
25. **Mixing shovels** (4 shovels) square nosed, shafts 90cm long.
26. **Knapping hammers** (5 hammers) 0.7kg weight, shaft 25cm long.
27. **Sledge hammers** (1 hammer) 3kg weight, shaft 60cm long.
28. **Sinkers hats** (2 hats) of lightweight fibre or plastic.
29. **Sieves** (2 sieves) round 20mm mesh for maximum size of concrete aggregate.
30. **Sieves** (2 sieves) round, 10mm mesh for maximum size of aggregate for porous concrete.
31. **Sieves** (2 sieves) round 5mm mesh for minimum size of aggregate.
32. **Sieves** (2 sieves) round, 3mm mesh for sand.
33. **Spare shafts** (12 shafts) 60cm long for mattock and picks.
34. **Headpans** (2 pans).
35. **Plumb bob** (1 bob) on plumb line.

C. HAND TOOLS

36. **Cutlasses** or matchets (1 cutlass).
37. **Cold chisels** (2 chisels) flat end, 25cm long, of 22mm hexagonal steel, for cutting reinforcing bars.
38. **Oil can** (1 can) 0.5 litre capacity, for headframe winding gear.
39. **Pliers** (1 pair) side cutting 20cm long.

40. **Wire brushes** (2 brushes).
41. **Spanners** (2 spanners) T head box spanners for 15mm nuts, for dismantling and assembling headframe.
42. **Spanners** (2 spanners) locknut, straight spanners for 12mm nuts (shuttering assembly).
43. **Spanners** (1 spanner) shifting, maximum opening 40mm.
44. **Mason's trowels** (1 trowel) 20cm blade.
45. **Level** (1 level) bricklayers.

D. LOCALLY MADE EQUIPMENT

46. **Top plumbing rod.** Made from timber or angle iron, 2.2m long with hook at centre for plumb line, and holes 15mm diameter drilled exactly 1 metre each side of the hook. A plumb line (carrying a plumb bob) will be attached to the hook.
47. **Long trimming rods** (1 set). Two rods 1.45m long, 12mm diameter, mild steel riveted together in the centre.
48. **Short trimming rods** (1 set). Two rods 1.30m long, 12mm diameter mild steel riveted together in centre.

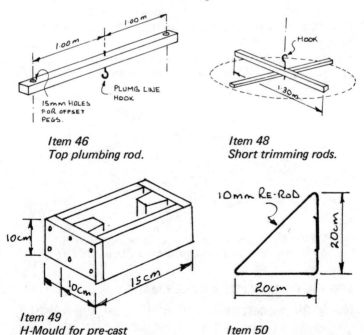

Item 46
Top plumbing rod.

Item 48
Short trimming rods.

Item 49
H-Mould for pre-cast concrete in-fill blocks.

Item 50
Curbs undercut gauge.

49. **H-Moulds** (6 moulds) for pre-cast concrete blocks for spaces between lifts. Blocks 10 x 10 x 15cm with recesses.
50. **Gauge** (1 gauge) for curb under cut, made from 8mm mild steel rod.
51. **Bosun's Chair** (1 chair) of 3cm timber for lowering on 12mm rope.

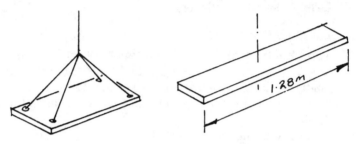

Item 51. Bosun's Chair.   *Item 52. Scaffold board.*

52. **Scaffold board** (1 board) of 3cm timber, 1.28m long, shaped to fit onto the ribs of lining shutters.
53. **Concrete scoop** (1 scoop) for pouring concrete behind lining.
54. **Gauge boxes** (2 boxes) of 2.5cm timber planks. One (for gravel) 75 x 75 x 30cm internal, one (for sand) 75 x 75 x 15cm internal.

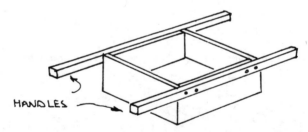

HANDLES

*Item 54. Aggregate gauge box. Open bottom —
75cm x 75cm x 30cm and 75cm x 75cm x 15cm.*

E. SPECIAL EQUIPMENT, LOCALLY MADE

55. **Mould for pre-cast caisson rings** (1 mould) 0.5 metre high, consisting of base plate, interior and exterior shutters, top and bottom templates. (See drawing in Chapter 9).

Threading the 15mm caisson connecting bolts

A supply of previously threaded 15mm diameter steel rods for connecting the caisson rings is usually obtained from a suitable workshop that has machine tools. Alternatively, the thread may be turned by hand using a suitable die cutter in the central store.

CHAPTER 19   NOTES ON THE USE OF EQUIPMENT AND SOME ALTERNATIVES

Item 1. Headframe

The specification and drawing in the schedule, (Chapter 18) is of a particular type of headframe. It is not possible to comment on the costs of this (or of other items) since these vary widely according to the time and place of purchase, but, as an indication, it is noted that in one area the cost of the headframe was estimated to be equivalent to about 25 metres of completed well.

Other designs of headframe are available, and the following are some points to note when making a selection:

The frame should be strong enough to deal with all loads without buckling, and at the same time should be capable of being dismantled into sections light enough to be carried by one man.

The legs (which should terminate in flat plates to prevent sinking into the ground when heavy loads are being carried) should be spaced far enough apart to prevent overturning if a caisson ring, weighing over 350kg, should start to swing.

The cross bracing at the two sides and at the end opposite the winch should allow sufficient headroom (1 metre is the absolute minimum) for handling of kibbles, pre-cast rings, shutters and other bulky items into and out of the well mouth.

If caisson rings are to be lowered it is most desirable that winch handles should be capable of being operated by two pairs of men, that a gearing with a ratio of about 3:1 should permit slow and accurate vertical movement of the load, and that a band brake should be fitted that will enable the heaviest load to be held independently of the winch handles. Without such a brake a brief period of inattention by a winchman may result in the load 'taking over' — once the handles start to spin it is almost impossible to get them under control, and there are recorded cases of men's ribs being broken while attempting to grab the turning handles under these circumstances.

To save time during the lowering of lighter loads (such as empty kibbles) it is useful to be able to disengage the gearing and rely entirely on the brake for control, but there must be a positive lock to prevent accidental disengagement at other times.

When purchasing or constructing headframes it is useful to obtain a supply of spare assembly bolts in case of loss during transport from site to site. These spares should not be kept at the well site otherwise they may be lost and be unavailable when the headframe is being re-erected at a new site.

Alternative headgear arrangements have been discussed in Part III and various other ingenious designs of lifting gear are in use — for example, frames made from tubular steel scaffolding. In any such arrangement the points made in the preceding paragraphs should be borne in mind and incorporated whenever possible. We would repeat, that for any programme of more than one or two wells it almost invariably pays in safety, in speed and in labour requirements to obtain a headframe of the same or similar type to that described.

Items 2, 3, and 4. Ropes

Steel ropes with fibre cores are undoubtedly the best for use with the headframes described. More rope can be accommodated on the winch; if properly maintained their additional length of life will more than compensate for the extra cost compared with hemp, nylon or other materials.

For makeshift headframes, especially for those using a brakepost as the method of control, steel ropes are less suitable. If they are used the men handling them during lowering should be provided with protective gloves, otherwise slight fraying can cause serious wounds to the hands

Nylon is a popular material for rope, but its elasticity is greater than hemp and accurate placing of heavy loads may be more difficult. It goes without saying that ropes, of whatever material, must be of adequate strength to carry the appropriate loads, and that regular inspection of all ropes (with particular attention being paid to the knots) must be made if accidents are to be avoided.

Items 5 and 6. Shuttering

In Chapter 20, details are given of a method of making lining shutters from locally available materials when one or two wells only are contemplated. As with headframes the additional cost of purpose-made equipment is quickly recovered in even a modest number of wells. The cost of a set of shutters 1m high is equivalent to the cost of about 3m of completed well.

The shutters described in the schedule are made of steel plate welded to rolled steel channel and angle iron. They should always be oiled before use (old automobile sump oil is quite adequate) and cleaned immediately they are removed from the concrete face. If any concrete adheres to them it should be removed with a wire brush (item 40) or by scraping — never by hammering.

When a new set of shutters is purchased it is common practice to cast a concrete block with a recess in the top to act as a template should the shutters later become distorted and require hammering out from the back side of the steel face. This template should be at a workshop or other central site rather than at a well site:--

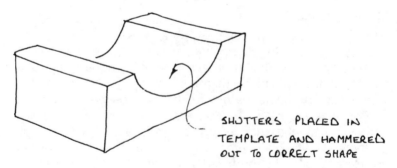

SHUTTERS PLACED IN TEMPLATE AND HAMMERED OUT TO CORRECT SHAPE

Template for reshaping shutters.

For large well sinking programmes it is usually worth while to have a heavy steel template made that can be carried from site to site for shutter maintenance. Where it is proposed to build up caissons on a cutting ring (as described in Chapter

186

Photo 75   Cutting Ring Mould – a) Interior sections.

Photo 76   – b) Exterior sections.

15), special shutters will be required for casting this ring, (Photos 75-76) and similar considerations will apply.

Items 7, 8 and 9. Wedges and bolts

These will normally be purchased with the shutters, the numbers shown are for the type illustrated. It usually pays to buy and hold a number of spares, but do not store them at the well site, otherwise they may be lost during the work.

Item 10. Kibbles

The use of kibbles has been described in Chapter 7. This is another item where it pays to purchase purpose-made equipment. Probably no other item will be exposed to such heavy wear and misuse, and durability is of great importance.

Item 11. Concreting buckets

A good projecting spout is essential for accurate placing of concrete.

Items 12-17. Clips and thimbles

These are for use with wire ropes, and are not only the strongest and safest means of fastening but will rapidly save their cost in reducing frayed ends. They should be regularly inspected to see that they are tightly fixed; this is especially important in the tropics where extremes of temperature may make them liable to slip.

Item 18. Tumbler hook

This may be made by the local blacksmith — the principle can be seen from the illustration. The load cannot free itself accidentally, but connection and disconnection is rapid. A common method of working is for the diggers to fill a kibble at the bottom of the well shaft. An emptied kibble is lowered, the tumbler hook is exchanged from empty to full kibble, and excavation continues into the former while the latter is wound to the surface for emptying.

Item 19. Miners bars

For loosening soil at the bottom of the shaft; may also be used for splitting rock at the surface when this is required for

188

aggregate. They are also needed for prising out small boulders from the shaft wall.

Item 20 and 21. Mattocks

The mattocks have blades at right angles to the line of their handles. The lighter (trimming) mattocks are for making a smooth finished surface to the shaft wall, against which concrete will subsequently be poured. These, and other tools used down the shaft, should have handles not more than 60cm long.

Items 22 and 23. Picks

The miner's picks (short handle, short cross piece) are for breaking hard surfaces at the side or bottom of the shaft ready for final trimming by mattock. The larger 'navvy's' pick is for use on the surface, excavating gravel or removing boulders.

Items 24 and 25. Shovels

Short handled, round nosed for use down the shaft; the actual shovel blade should be small enough to fill material into the kibble. The square nosed shovels are for use on the surface, loading sand and gravel into gauge boxes, mixing and loading concrete into buckets or moulds. Whether these have long (over 1 metre) or normal (90cm) handles is a matter of local choice and custom.

Item 26. Knapping hammers

For breaking stone for concrete aggregate.

Item 27. Sledge hammer

For splitting rock or boulders in the well, breaking up outcrop rock for aggregate, and for use with cold chisels. (Item 37).

Item 28. Sinkers safety hats

A most important safety precaution; two is the minimum number required in a team, but it is common practice in many areas for each sinker to have (and be responsible for) his own hat.

Items 29-32. Sieves

Round sieves are specified for testing and grading sand and aggregate. Many countries prefer the use of flat sieves, operated by two men, in frames similar to shallow aggregate gauge boxes suspended by ropes from an overhead framework. These are more economial of labour when a considerable quantity of aggregate is needed.

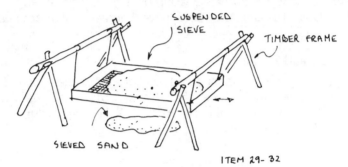

Suspended sieve.

Item 33. Spare shafts

It is usually false economy to try and use local 'bush' poles for tool handles — in any case the time wasted in cutting, trimming and fitting is often of more value than the cost of the shaft.

Item 34. Headpans

In areas where wheelbarrows are commonly used one of these should be provided for handling gravel and sand, but there should always be at least one headpan (or similar receptacle) for measuring small quantities of material, e.g. sand and cement for mortar.

Item 35. Plumb bob

Not perhaps essential (an iron nut or similar weight will serve) but the cord to which it is attached should be reserved for plumbing alone, kept free from knots, unravelling or fraying, and wound onto a reel or former (see illustration in Chapter 7). A purpose-made plumb bob tends to keep its line from misuse better than a makeshift one does.

Item 36. Cutlass or matchet

For site clearance, and numerous minor jobs.

Item 37. Cold chisels

For cutting reinforcement (a hacksaw or proper cutters are sometimes preferred), and can often be effective (with the sledge hammer) in splitting small boulders that intrude into the well shaft. They are also useful for trimming mixing shovels that have become sharp and dangerous due to wear.

Item 38. Oil can

The headframe winding gear, including the headsheaves, should be kept regularly lubricated — don't forget that oil must also be provided.

Item 39. Pliers

Principally for use with soft iron binding wire to bind together re-rods in reinforcement cages.

Item 40. Wire brushes

For cleaning shuttering and tools, and for removing any scale on re-rods.

Items 41-43. Spanners

Sizes will be specified to suit the bolt sizes used on head-frames, shuttering, winch and pulley fastenings.

Item 44. Mason's trowel

For pointing between lifts and rendering wellhead, apron and any other exposed concrete.

Item 45. Bricklayer's level

For setting lining shutters and caisson rings, also for grading apron and ensuring verticality of headwall.

Items 46-48. Plumbing and trimming rods

Already described in Part II. Can be made of timber, but are more durable and convenient when made of metal.

Item 49. Moulds for H-Blocks

Six moulds are shown in the schedule: it is worth having at

least this number so that blocks may be made whenever the surface labourers have a slack period.

Item 50. Undercut gauge

Made of 8mm re-rod when this is the only thickness used on site, but is more rigid and durable when made of thicker material (say 10mm or 12mm).

Items 51 and 52. Bosun's chair and scaffold board

Work on all shutters above the lowest two in a lift have to be carried out from a temporary platform; this work includes setting shutters, fastening reinforcement, pouring and tamping concrete, pointing infill blocks. Until the shutters are bolted together and rigid the bosun's chair must be used, suspended from the main winding rope. The same arrangement should be used by sinkers for ascending and descending when the well is deeper than the first lift; from the bosun's chair, too, detailed inspection can be made of the completed well shaft.

While the shutters are still in place it is somewhat simpler to use an accurately cut scaffold board resting on the shuttering ribs, but great care must be taken that the ends of the board do not get damaged, reducing the safety margin of an already small overlap.

Item 53. Concrete scoop

A simple chute, made from beaten-out roofing metal or similar material, to assist in pouring concrete behind lining shutters. Without it wastage of concrete during pouring is almost inevitable, even using concreting buckets with good spouts.

Item 54. Gauge boxes

The use of gauge boxes for aggregate and sand has been described; for accurate measurement the box must lie flat on the mixing slab and the material must be loaded into it by shovel or headpan until the surface is flat and level with the top of the box.

Boxes of the size shown will produce approximately 1/6 cubic metre (170 litres) of concrete per filling, for which purpose 50kg cement (34 litres) are required. If (as is usual) the cement is available in 50kg sacks, no special gauging box is required for this material, but if it is supplied in bulk or in other units than a 34 litre measure (either gauge box or other receptacle) will be necessary.

Item 55. Caisson ring moulds

The various parts of the mould and fittings are described and illustrated in Chapter 9. While it is possible to make these of timber and plywood it will certainly pay, when several wells are to be constructed, to have them fabricated of steel plate on rolled angle iron or channel ribs.

Although only one mould is shown in the schedule the provision of two or three may prove to be a wise investment in time saved. This particularly applies in relatively shallow wells where the time spent on the sinking and lining of the section above the aquifer is insufficient to build up a stock of caisson rings and have them cured in time for insertion in the intake. The steel caisson mould is built to a similar pattern to the main shaft lining shutters; the holes to insert the pegs to make seepage holes are drilled after the sections have been constructed.

CHAPTER 20 MAKING LOW COST SHUTTERS FROM LOCALLY AVAILABLE MATERIAL

Steel plate and rolled channel sections, cut to shape and welded together, make strong, durable shutters. If you are planning a large well programme lasting several years, then the high initial cost of these steel shutters can be spread across each well, and will contribute only a very small fraction of the total cost of each well. Drawings and photographs of sectional circular steel shutters that bolt together down the well, are shown in some detail in Chapter 18.

If however, you intend to construct only one or two wells, then it is usually prohibitively expensive to have steel shutters especially made up. In this case, low cost shutters made from locally available materials such as timber, plywood, salvaged sheet metal, etc., should be considered.

These consist of the usual framing ribs which support the weight of the concrete, and a sheet of lining material fastened outside the ribs to contain the concrete as it sets. There are many ways to make low cost shutters, the one shown in Photos 78-84 was made up from scrap plywood as an example.

a) The first step is to draw up the required shape of the ribs — the outside radius of the ribs being the finished internal radius of the well less the thickness of the lining sheet. The easiest way to do this is to draw up the complete circular shape of the rib section on the ground on a paper or cardboard template. The template is divided up into quarters which form each section of the shutters, the template being then cut out and transferred onto the rib material.

b) The ribs may be made from plywood, or sections of timber glued or screwed together. The rib templates are traced onto the plywood or timber and the ribs cut out; a 0.5 metre section has two ribs, and one metre deep set of shutters usually has three horizontal ribs.

c) Vertical stringers from plywood or timber to form the edges of each shutter section are cut out to shape and glued or screwed to the ribs. It is helpful at this stage to assemble the glued shutter frame in order to check that the vertical stringers will fit flush together. The holes for the holding bolts can now be drilled.

d) The shutter lining sheet may be made of plywood, sheet steel, or even narrow planks which are bevelled at the sides to fit flush together. The lining is cut to shape, bent around the shutter frames, and nailed, screwed or glued into place. This may be done whilst the frame is bolted together, or with the frame held securely in a simple jig.

e) When the shutters are finished, they are planed or rasped smooth and painted or oiled to repel water.

It is essential that timber shutters are treated carefully as they are being lowered into and out of the well. They should not be vibrated by a hammer to compact the poured concrete, or to jar them loose when the concrete has set, otherwise they will quickly begin to fall apart. These shutters can be made very substantial and sturdy — solid timber shutters, carefully assembled, glued, oiled and handled, will last during the construction of many wells.

It is possible to line a well using only a single set of shutters. In this case only a metre of the lining is poured at a time, this reduces the cost of the shuttering but makes work very slow as the shuttering ring has to be left in place for several days to allow the concrete to set. In a large scale well construction programme there are usually more than 5 sets of shutters for each well, these are left in place after the concrete has been poured in each lift, and a further 5 metres of excavation removed from the well bottom and taken out inside the shutters. For only one or two wells, with one set of shutters, you will have to balance the extra time of construction against the extra cost of building several sets of shutters which will only be used a few times.

The principle described above can equally be applied to the fabrication of a caisson ring mould, in which case both interior and exterior shutters will be needed as well as a base plate and templates to hold the bolts, tubes and spacers in place during casting.

Photo 77 *Constructing Low Cost Timber Shutters —*
a) Drawing the ribs — these are marked out on the material which will be used to make the ribs.

Photo 78
b) Assemble shutter frame, the r┊ and vertical stringers are glued together. Check that frame will fit flush together — try bolts.

Photo 79
c) Checking frame holding bolts.

Photo 80
d) Shutter frame.

Photo: John Collett

Photo 81 Constructing Low Cost Timber Shutters—
e) Simple jig to hold frame whilst lining sheet is added.

Photo 83   g) Finished and assembled shutter. Note wedged panel for easy assembly and dismantling.

Photo 82
f) Adding lining sheet to assembled frame.

Photo 84
h) A cheap and simple set of shutters used to make pre-cast concrete rings.

CHAPTER 21   CONCRETE

Throughout this manual the use of concrete has been recommended for a number of purposes, especially for well shaft lining, caisson rings and for well head construction.

Concrete is a particularly useful and adaptable material. It is versatile, capable of being made and used by relatively unskilled workers, is labour intensive and incorporates locally available material in its composition, is plastic when initially mixed and is sufficiently slow in setting to allow adequate time to lay it in its final position during its plastic stage. It is durable under almost all conditions and has a virtually unlimited life.

It has certain disadvantages, which are easily overcome if they are understood and provided for. During its initial setting period it is weak and easily damaged; protection is needed for the first day or two, during which time the new concrete should not be required to bear a load. Even after setting is complete (after a month or more) it is very much weaker in tension than in compression; to overcome this it is 'reinforced', i.e. steel rods are incorporated at carefully planned points to deal with stresses due to tension. Its slow chemical setting action can be upset if it is allowed to dry out too quickly; 'curing', or keeping the surfaces protected from direct sunlight or drying winds by covering them with wet sacking or other material, is the best preventative.

In the foregoing chapters the practical considerations have been referred to in some detail without any reason being given as to why certain precautions are necessary. The present chapter is an attempt to deal with some of these theoretical points, necessarily very briefly.

The basic components of concrete are cement, water and aggregate. When steel is incorporated also the concrete is said to be reinforced.

Cement

It is not proposed to go into the chemical properties of the cement, which will have to be purchased and must be assumed to be of adequate quality. Ordinary Portland Cement is the grade normally used in well sinking; in certain types of soil 'sulphate-resistant' or other special grades may be called for, but this requirement is likely to be generally known in the areas concerned. Other 'quick-setting' grades may be available, but are unlikely to be used in normal well construction practice; not only are such cements more expensive than ordinary Portland grade but they may need different mixing and laying techniques.

Cement has a natural affinity for water, as soon as it becomes wet the chemical reaction which is the basis of its 'setting' starts and it becomes useless for making concrete if it is not used within half an hour or so. Even when not directly in contact with water it may absorb sufficient moisture from damp air to produce the same effect. Hence cement must be stored before use in waterproof containers, under cover, not in direct contact with the ground. Once a sack or other container is opened any cement remaining unused should be protected by being wrapped in plastic or put into a metal container; similar precautions are necessary if the sack becomes damaged. If any cement is found to be hard or lumpy, possibly as a result of getting wet while being transported, it should on no account be used for concrete where strength is required, (e.g. in well linings or caisson rings). If it is not too badly affected it might be suitable for the apron surround, but generally speaking it should be scrapped.

Water

Cement is usually expensive because it is of a high degree of purity and is therefore capable of developing high strength. If it is mixed with impure water, containing clay, mud, oil or salts, the quality of the cement is to a large degree wasted since its strength will be reduced. Unless there is an existing well near to the sinking site water for concrete mixing will have to be brought to the mixing slab in containers (often old oil drums). It is important that these are thoroughly cleaned before use, and that the water is drawn from a clean source.

As a rule of thumb it may be said that if the water is not fit for drinking it is not suitable for making concrete.

Aggregate

Aggregate is the term used for the mixture of different sizes of stone that form the body of the concrete. Ideally the stone would be so graded that the smaller sizes exactly fitted into the spaces between the larger ones so that no gaps were left in the mass. Sometimes a natural gravel can be found where this desirable state is approached, but a much more common condition calls for the mixing of large and small stones in suitable proportions to achieve the same result. The smaller size stones together comprise sand; sand used for concreting is usually best obtained from a river bed. It should be clean, sharp and free from clay or loam.

The larger size stones form the bulk of the concrete and give it its strength. Obviously they cannot do this unless they are themselves strong and resistant to crushing. Some of the strongest concrete is made from gravel — stones rounded by the natural action of water and weather — and where there are suitable deposits of such gravel in the neighbourhood these are likely to be the most suitable sources of aggregate. Another source, much used, is outcrop rock, but this must be 'knapped' or broken to convenient size with light hammers after having been split from the outcrop with sledge hammer and chisel. Such aggregate known as 'broken stone', can be very successful, but one danger is that the outer surface of softer, weathered rock is often included to the detriment of the concrete strength.

In areas where neither gravel nor stone is easily available, such substitute materials as coral, laterite or calcite may be obtainable — in the absence of these it may be possible to use broken burnt bricks. The points to watch for are hardness (individual pieces should be capable of being cracked and split, but not crushed or powdered, by a blow from a knapping hammer), cleanliness (the aggregate should be free from clay, loam and organic matter) and grading. As regards grading the individual pieces should all pass through a 20mm sieve and be retained on a 5mm mesh. Above all, all powder should be removed and if this cannot be done by sieving the aggregate should be washed before use.

The mixture

Various proportions of the concrete mixture are called for by different uses; in this manual two only are quoted. For lining, normal caisson rings, wellheads and miscellaneous use a 1:2.5:5 (cement:sand:gravel) mix is used, while for intakes where porous concrete is needed the proportion is 1:1:4. Note: for simplicity the larger element of the aggregate (whether this consists of stone, brick or other substitute) will be called 'gravel', while the smaller element will be referred to as 'sand', even though this may be crushed coral or other alternative.

It should be noted that 1 measure of cement plus 2.5 measures of sand plus 5 measures of aggregate do not produce 8.5 measures of concrete. As the sand enters the spaces between the gravel particles and the cement fills the pores in the sand 1 + 2.5 + 5 equals approximately 5 in this instance. In other words if the volume of concrete required is known the volume of gravel needed will be the same, with one half the amount of sand and one fifth the volume of cement. It is because of this complication that it is desirable to adhere to one standard mix, for which gauge boxes and an easily identified quantity of cement can be used. Since 50kg of loose cement occupies 34 litres (i.e. 1.45kg per litre) the quantities contained in the gauge boxes are respectively 2.5 and 5 times this amount.

When water is added the volume of the concrete increases by a small amount (much less than the volume of water added since there is still space within the mixture into which the water can enter) but as the concrete sets and dries out it will shrink a little so the additional volume due to the water may be ignored.

The 'twice-dry-twice wet' method of mixing has been described in Chapter 7. Two separate effects result from this. Firstly, during the dry mixes, the sand enters into the gravel spaces and the cement into the sand pores as described above. Until this has been done no water should be added; if inspection shows that mixing is incomplete (e.g. that the cement is not evenly spread throughout the mass, or one part is sandier than another) an additional dry mix is needed.

When the water is added this combines with the cement to form a 'slurry', and it is this slurry that will bind the particles together. For the concrete to reach its full strength it is essential that every particle of gravel or sand should be coated evenly with this slurry so that there is an adhesive bond in every direction. It is for this reason that oil, clay or other contaminants are so harmful; they prevent the slurry reaching and adhering to the surface of the particles.

Provided that the dry mixing was thoroughly carried out, with the cement evenly distributed through the mass, two wet mixes should be sufficient to distribute the slurry to every particle.

When the wet concrete mix is 'handled', i.e. when it is shovelled into buckets, transported, poured or spread, the particles tend to separate, and this separation must be kept to the minimum possible. Another source of weakness may be the entrainment of bubbles of air during pouring. To counter-act both these faults is is usual to 'tamp' concrete as it is poured behind shutters, i.e. to stir and vibrate it with a piece of steel rod. When pouring into a mould on the surface (for caisson rings or H-blocks) tamping may be combined with shaking or tapping the mould with wooden blocks. Open-laid concrete, such as the drainage apron, may be worked with the shovel or tamped on the surface with the edge of a board to achieve the same effect.

Reference has been made to 1:1:4 mixture porous concrete. Because only a small quantity of sand is included the adhesive effect of the cement slurry can only be produced where the gravel particles actually touch, hence the strength of the final concrete will be much less than a normal mix and more care must be taken in handling both before and after setting. When the water dries out during the setting process a series of inter-connected pores will form channels through the concrete, permitting water to pass but forming a 'strainer' to keep back solid particles.

Reinforcement

To strengthen concrete where it is weakest — in tension—mild steel rods, called 're-rods' in this manual, are incorporated. The theory behind their placing and calculations of their size are outside the scope of these notes; the practical results of these calculations have been incorporated into the manual.

For simplicity a single size of reinforcing rod has been

shown for all uses (except for such special purposes as the caisson connecting bolts). This avoids the possibility of confusion when different diameter rods are stored on a site. 8mm diameter is a convenient size, easy to bend and cut; anything smaller is difficult to manage being too flexible. If 8mm is not easily obtainable 10mm may be used instead, using two rods for every three shown.

Re-rod must be completely embedded in concrete otherwise it will rust away in time. It must be placed exactly in accordance with the directions given — one centimetre out of position can make a material difference to the strength of a lining or caisson ring. The steel in the concrete must be coated with the cement slurry over its whole surface to ensure a bond with the concrete. For this reason the rods must be kept clean, free from mud or oil, and any loose rust or scale that may have formed due to careless storage must be removed with a wire brush before laying. Ends should be hooked (as described) and rods should be fastened together by binding tightly with soft iron binding wire.

To avoid voids and air pockets around the re-rods during pouring, the wet concrete should be tamped as described above, but great care must be taken during this operation that the position of the reinforcement 'cage' within the concrete is not disturbed.

PART V   ADDITIONAL INFORMATION

CHAPTER 22 WATER LIFTING FROM HAND DUG WELLS

The choice, design, construction, operation, maintenance and repair of water lifting devices is a large subject that cannot be adequately covered in a chapter of this manual. Nevertheless, water lifting from hand dug wells has distinct advantages and features that are often overlooked and some of these are outlined in this chapter. Hand dug wells, because of their relatively shallow penetration into the aquifer, should be expected to yield only modest amounts of water unless the well yield has been improved by the methods described in Chapter 17.

Water lifting by hand for domestic use

The traditional rope and bucket is the equipment most often used to lift the small amounts of water needed for domestic purposes. The water container is either improvised from local materials, such as bamboo with a rope made from similar local materials or is a purchased galvanised iron bucket with a handle. Generally, each well user has his or her own rope and bucket which increases greatly the risk that the well will become contaminated from waste material carried into the well on the bucket.

A communal rope and bucket that is a permanent installation on the well is a great improvement (see Chapter 10) and should be encouraged wherever possible.

Local innovations that are usually ignored because of their lack of glamour should be seriously considered. The example shown in Photos 85-86 shows 2 litre rubber buckets on wire handles that are locally made in Upper Volta and sell for less than one tenth of the cost of a galvanised iron bucket. These lift small quantities of water comfortably and do not tip the water out if the bucket swings against the side of the well during lifting. Most important, the collapsible buckets cannot

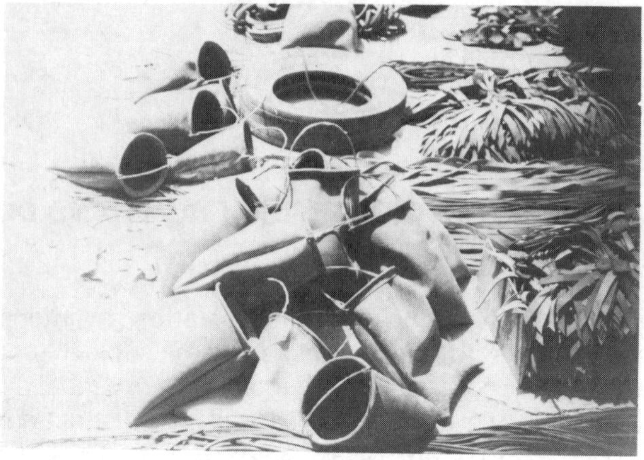

Photo 85   A local innovation -- the collapsible rubber
bucket. Locally produced 2 litre rubber buckets, sold in
the market. -- Upper Volta.

Photo 86   These cheap collapsible rubber buckets cannot
stand upright on the ground either at the wellhead or in
the house. Risks of contaminated water being carried into
the well are therefore reduced. The buckets cannot be
used for cooking. -- Upper Volta.

be rested on the ground without spilling their contents either in the house or by the well and this will reduce substantially the risks of contaminated matter being carried on the bucket into the well water. The buckets are usually hung from ceiling or wall hooks in the house, out of the reach of animals.

Sealing the mouth of the well with a properly designed concrete slab will completely protect the well from surface contamination. In this case a mechanical pump of some sort is needed. These have a sorry record of breakage in many areas due to poor maintenance and a great deal of work is underway in different countries to improve the pumps. Examples of these are shown in Photos 87-89 and further information may be obtained from the World Health Organisation (see Chapter 25). Handpumps with rotary cranks, although more expensive, are found to be more durable than the lever action crank because if the pump is used too vigorously, the rotary crank will simply overspeed instead of hammering violently against the stops, which occurs with the lever action type.

In a number of countries wooden handles and beams are used. Although these are not necessarily more durable than the metal components, they are cheap initially and can be easily repaired by the local carpenters. It is found too, that when the repair is a local responsibility, misuse is discouraged.

Water lifting for small scale irrigation or stock rearing by animal or motor powered pumps

The large diameter of hand dug wells allows bulky water lifting machines to be used, such as the chain and washer pump, the shadoof, etc. These wells can of course be surface pumped by diesel or electric powered equipment, but the larger diameter allows the traditional devices to be used as a standby in case the diesel engine breaks down.

This is of great importance for areas remote from repair or spares facilities, where the loss of a motor powered pump will threaten crops and the lives of animals. It must be stressed however that most hand dug wells will not yield very large volumes of water and it is quite possible that a motor powered pump will empty the well faster than water can flow

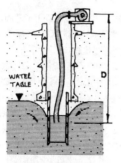
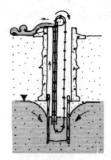

CENTRIFUGAL PUMP AT
WELL HEAD . DEPTH 'D'
NOT GREATER THAN 8m.

LARGE DIAMETER
CHAIN PUMP IN WELL.

Choice of pumping equipment in large diameter wells.

in; this is likely to cause the movement of sediment from the aquifer into the well, and possible collapse of the well lining. Over-pumping the well can be prevented by suspending the suction pipe or pump unit at the appropriate depth below the water table.

Since pump efficiency is always improved by keeping suction lifts as small as possible, there are advantages in setting centrifugal pumps at the bottom of the well: this is possible only when the diameter of the shaft is large enough. Bulky centrifugal pumps are usually considerably cheaper

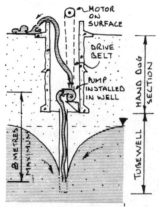
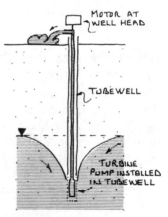

CENTRIFUGAL PUMP AT BASE OF
HAND DUG SECTION EXTRACTING
WATER FROM TUBEWELL

TURBINE PUMP IN TUBE WELL
DRIVEN FROM THE SURFACE

Hand dug section allows a bulky centrifugal pump to be used.

Photo 87 Improved Water Well Pumps —
a) 'Abi' type pump made overstrength to
withstand constant use. This pump is
expensive but is an improvement on
the standard commercial types. —
Senegal.

Photo 88 b) 'Vergnet' type well pump
operated by footpower. The ropes and
hydraulic working parts are made
of plastic and can be very quickly
replaced. The pump works on
hydraulic transmission and the only
wearing part is the foot piston. —
Upper Volta.

Photo 89 c) 'Jalna' type pump can be made from welded
or hand forged parts using local craftsmen and materials. —
India.

than the small diameter turbine pumps needed to fit into small diameter boreholes.

In parts of India, tubewells into the aquifer are completed with a hand dug section from the surface to the water table. The pump is fitted at the base of the well where access is easy and powered by a belt drive from a motor at the surface. The suction pipe is lowered into the tubewell, which can be up to 7 metres or so deep into the aquifer. It has been found that the extra cost of hand digging the top section of well (even through rock) is saved by the lower cost of the centrifugal pump.

Water lifting by wind power

Wind powered water pumps are widely used in many parts of the world and although the larger commercial machines are designed to lift water from depths of hundreds of metres, smaller machines either locally or commercially made, can be used to pump shallow hand dug wells. In the latter case, hand dug wells have distinct advantages over small diameter tubewells, namely the large volume of stored water and the more rapid inflow for the same drawdown. The power of a wind machine varies as the cube of the speed of the wind. This means that if the speed of the wind doubles, then the power output will increase not twice, but *eight times.* At the higher wind speeds the machines are designed to cut out, but at the lower wind speeds, which give the least power yet blow over far the longest periods over the year, the wind machine, water pump and water well must be designed to give the best performance possible.

The wind does not blow steadily at one speed; even over a period of minutes or even seconds the speed and therefore the power of the wind will vary greatly. It is during the short but strongest gusts that the wind machine will pump the most water. During these short periods, it is critical for efficient operation to have the water table in the well as near to the surface as possible; the larger volume of stored water in a hand dug well is drawn down relatively slowly compared to the small volume of water stored in a tubewell.

The energy of the short gusts is therefore used to lift a larger volume of water a short distance. In a tubewell, on the other hand, the water is quickly pumped out and unless

212

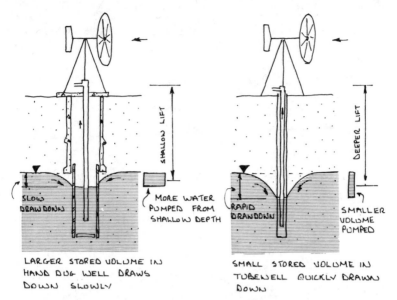

LARGER STORED VOLUME IN
HAND DUG WELL DRAWS
DOWN SLOWLY

SMALL STORED VOLUME IN
TUBEWELL QUICKLY DRAWN
DOWN

*Water pumping from hand dug and small diameter wells
during the same gust of wind. In both cases, the wells are
re-charged by inflowing ground water in the calmer periods.
An example of a cheap, locally made, wind machine built
from timber and iron, with cloth sails, is shown below.*

*Photo 90   Partly rigged cretan sail windwheel pumping
water to greenhouses growing cash crops.*

inflow is exceptionally rapid the energy from the gust will be expended lifting smaller amounts of water from greater depths.

In both cases, the wells are re-charged by inflowing ground water in the calmer periods.

An example of a cheap, locally made, wind machine built from timber and iron, with cloth sails, is shown in Photo 90.

CHAPTER 23   THE COSTS OF SELF-HELP, HAND-DUG WELL CONSTRUCTION PROGRAMMES

In this chapter, the various elements of a self–help well construction programme that determine the final costs of the completed wells are considered in greater detail. An example taken from an actual programme in West Africa for the year 1973-74 is presented with costs broken down into percentage terms. These figures indicate that the major proportion of the costs of the programme lay in the management and in the supplies of materials and equipment. Heavy administration costs are typical for programmes of this sort and show clearly how construction techniques that can be tackled without constant supervision allow the organisers to concentrate on the smooth delivery of materials to the well sites and the planning and motivation within the villages, which is an essential part of the work. Examining the costs against similar costs of a programme using smaller diameter boreholes constructed in the same year by the same organisation shows clearly that the small diameter wells cost one half as much again as the hand dug wells because the programme organisers were tied up directly supervising the technical work. These costs are shown aggregated below, and are also compared with the costs of a programme operated by a local Government Department using hand dug wells, but including air compressors, pneumatic tools and water pumps; this equipment caused much trouble through the difficulties of maintenance and accounts for the higher costs.

The high administration costs can of course be shared over a number of different projects at each well site using similar materials and the same equipment at very little extra cost. For instance, the lining shutters can provide the formwork for making thin-walled 'ferro-cement' grain bins and water tanks in the village at which the well is being built. Extra cement can be used to make cattle slaughtering slabs,

215

hygienic toilets for the market place, etc. The multiple use of equipment and skills will dramatically reduce the cost of each project and forms part of what is known by economists as 'integrated development'.

Name of Organisation	Method of self help construction	Construction cost $/m	%	Administration cost $/m	%	Total cost $/m	%
P.C. Volunteers	Hand dug wells, no machines	28.9	41.4	41.2	58.6	70.1	100
Upper Volta Rural Develop- ment Org.	Hand dug wells, air compressors and motor powered winch. Excavation mainly by well users. (Est. from 1974-5 programme).	48	55	42	45	90	100
P.C. Volunteers	Small diameter tube wells, man powered	41.5	38.4	66.5	61.6	108	100

A description of the costs

The final annual costs of each well programme and the cost of each constructed well will vary greatly according to local conditions and the efficiency with which the programme is managed.

a) Materials used in construction

The costs of the cement and steel rod reinforcement needed to construct the wells is one of the largest items in the programme. These materials will often need to be imported and carried great distances and the cost of these will therefore increase with the distance from the supply source. Enquiries will have to be made locally about available sources of supply. In difficult and remote areas transportation costs are often greater than the initial purchase cost of the materials and this may even make the choice of reinforced concrete hand dug wells a poor one.

Using locally available materials, consistent with strength, durability and soundness, will help to reduce the costs of the well. Some examples of local materials are given in this manual — using brick, masonry, timber, bamboo and hemp rope etc., and even locally worked metals may be employed.

216

Innovation in the use of materials should be carefully and sympathetically considered. There are many examples of local innovations working satsifactorily in practice, despite having been earlier disregarded by trained experts. Allowance should be made in the estimates of cost for wastage losses in transportation, storage and use.

b) Tools and equipment

The tools and equipment needed for the construction of hand dug wells have already been described in chapters 18 and 19 of this manual. If only single, isolated wells are planned, it can be prohibitively expensive to purchase or have made up sturdy well built equipment and in this case temporary local materials should be improvised wherever possible, consistent with safety. A larger programme however, will allow the high initial costs of equipment to be spread over all of the wells and in this case cheap equipment is a false economy. Multiple use of the equipment over different projects will also allow the costs to be spread.

Simple tools and equipment that can be used by relatively unskilled people will save a great deal of time and trouble in training, instruction and maintenance but this does not necessarily mean that the equipment is in any way inferior.

c) Transporting the materials and equipment

Many inhabited areas of the world are very poorly provided with vehicular access. This will often restrict the transportation of materials and equipment to sizes that can be carried by hand. Heavy equipment is a special problem unless it can be dismantled; servicing motor powered equipment is also difficult in isolated areas or in areas where efficient maintenance and repair facilities for machinery are not yet developed.

In very isolated regions the cost of transportation will often be greater than the initial purchase cost and this factor can decide the technique of well construction that must be adopted.

d) Employment of local artisans and the contribution of self-help work by the users

The employment of local artisans skilled in some or all

aspects of hand dug well construction work will allow the programme organisers to concentrate on the difficult task of managing the efficient delivery of materials and equipment. These artisans can, with some training, manage the day-to-day construction work on each well, can organise the work of the well users in collecting sand and gravel for the concrete lined wells and ensure that excavation and lining is technically satisfactory. It is of great value to employ skilled local men who are respected in the community. Those who have already worked in traditional well sinking work will understand the major problems and how they can be overcome. Training local artisans will provide important future benefits as they will have the knowledge and confidence to improve other wells in their areas.

A large self-help programme should consider employing trained artisans on a permanent basis and perhaps also employ complete well sinking teams during the programme. In this case, the work of the local people who will use the well will consist of collecting concrete aggregate or other materials and providing shelter for the well sinking teams.

The great advantage of self-help schemes is that they allow the local people to provide the foundations for their material development by their own efforts without spending scarce capital resources. Many farmers and people in small villages have periods of the year when they are not pressed by other work commitments. It is during these periods that they can find time for improving their water supplies either for domestic use or for irrigation.

e,f) The planning and administration of self-help programmes

If the well users knew how to do the work, were able to organise themselves and had the materials and equipment or the confidence, it is probable that they would already have constructed safe and efficient wells. These vital factors are often lacking and it is the task of the programme organisers to take on the role of development worker as well as technical assistant to overcome these limitations at the lowest possible cost. The cost of planning and administering these programmes is likely to be the largest fraction of the total costs and as we have already suggested, hand dug wells allow skills of organisation to be spread out over a larger number of these wells than would be possible if small diameter wells were chosen.

The programme should include the education of the well users in the need for hygiene both at the well and in their homes. Ideally, the well construction programme should be part of a wider programme of development covering sanitation, improved agriculture, hygiene and general education etc.

g)   Exploring for ground water and choosing the well site

These factors have already been considered in Part I of this manual, and it is not necessary to add to this except to emphasise that exploration for ground water must in some areas be one of the most important parts of the programme. The failure to find water in the well is both costly and demoralising to the well users and sinkers who are doing most of the laborious construction work.

In some difficult well sinking areas, for instance in the weathered basalts of the Indian Deccan, geophysical exploration techniques are essential to increase the likelihood of locating the well directly above one of the leached fissures that both lie below the ground and are likely to hold ground water. The costs of the exploration teams and their equipment is spread out over all of the wells in these difficult areas and their cost is usually less than one tenth of the final cost of each well. Failure to find ground water in this area often led to as many as four dry wells out of five before geophysical exploration was adopted. If only a few isolated wells are to be constructed however, then the cost of these techniques can be prohibitive.

An alternative method of groundwater exploration uses rigs which drill cheap, small diameter holes for investigation purposes only — the holes are then abandoned. A hand auger or driven well can also be used for this purpose if the ground conditions are suitable. One advantage of hand dug wells is that they can, in stable soils, be excavated down without lining, possibly using timber cribbing, to see if water is present at a reasonable depth; they can then be abandoned without the waste of expensive materials if water is not found.

219

h) Maintenance costs after construction

It is essential that the need for maintaining the well in a clean, sound and sanitary condition is carefully explained to the users before the well is completed. This maintenance will almost inevitably be left to the well users. The cost of providing official teams to travel around rural areas looking after the wells is usually prohibitive. One reason for encouraging self-help well construction is the strong likelihood that if the well was requested in the first place by the users and if they have taken part in its construction, they will consider themselves responsible for its upkeep. This is particularly true if the top is sealed and a mechanical pump of some sort is fitted.

The year account for a self-help hand dug well construction programme in West Africa, 1973-4 — a case study:

1. Programme: P.C.V., Upper Volta, West Africa, 1973-4. The programme was arranged to integrate with the work of the Upper Voltain Government Rural Water Supply Department; 12 volunteers were working on the wells in 8 regions, with Ouagadougou acting as the administrative centre. Each volunteer managed the construction of over 20 wells during the season.

2. Wells constructed: 206 new wells constructed, average depth = 9m; maximum depth = 45m; minimum depth = 5m.

   91 old wells were renovated and deepened

   Total concrete lining = 1988 metres

3. Dimensions of wells:

Main lining	Internal diameter	=	1.40 m
	Wall thickness	=	7.50 cm
Caisson lining	Internal diameter	=	1.00 m
	Wall thickness	=	11.00 cm
Wellhead wall	Internal diameter	=	1.40 m
	Wall thickness	=	10.00 cm
Apron	Thickness	=	15.00 cm
	Width	=	1.00 m

4. Personnel: Peace Corps Volunteers — live in the regions and organise supplies, materials, equipment and tools and supervise programmes.

   Masons — employed locally, these skilled artisans work

on the construction of the wells, supervising the excavation and concreting work.

Well users — the local people work on a voluntary basis doing most of the labouring, excavation, collecting aggregate etc.

5. Climate: Upper Volta is part of the Sahelian drought zone with a short rainy season and a long dry season. Well digging stops during the wet season when the well users are busy with their agriculture. Communications are poor but access to most villages was possible in the dry season along dirt roads.

6. Geology: Most of the wells were constructed through hard laterite soils that had to be picked out by hand without using explosives. The aquifer consisted of sandy material. In the wet season the water table rises to within 3 metres of the surface.

7. Cost of well construction: The various costs of the programme for the year 1973-4 are shown in the following table. In order to arrive at a true cost of the programme for the year it is necessary to consider all of the costs involved, both construction and administration costs.

The administration costs including office expenses, overheads and the salaries and lodging allowances for the volunteers amounted to nearly 59% of the total costs. Transportation of personnel and materials from the base stores in Ouagadougou to the regional stores where the well programmes were being carried out amounted to 15% of the total costs.

Tools and equipment cost less than 3%, indicating the economies that can be gained if the cost of the equipment can be spread over many wells. The materials to construct the wells came to 22% of the total costs. The largest proportion of costs arose from the administration of the scheme and the salaries of the Peace Corps Volunteers. These salaries are equivalent to those paid by the Upper Voltain Rural Water Supply Programme to its own well organisers. This latter programme was more costly (see table in the introduction to this chapter) because the wells were larger in diameter, 1.80 metres internal diameter compared with the 1.30 diameter P.C.V. wells, and compressors needed a great deal of maintenance and caused much delay. The P.C.V.'s programme was comparatively cheaper but did not penetrate the aquifer to as great a depth. Some idea of the value of the work contributed voluntarily by the well users can be deduced from these figures. The U.V. programme employed self-contained teams of well constructors and the local people contributed only the aggregate and some of the haulage of some of the equipment; each team had an air compressor and tools available, a lorry to transport equipment, a fabricated steel headframe and powered lifting tackle. The Peace Corps programme, on the other hand, had a minimum of equipment and relied almost completely on the work of the well users in the construction of the well.

The costs in the table quoted below indicate that substantial savings can be made in the cost of well construction if the use of expensive equipment is kept to a minimum and substituted by the labour of the well users.

P.C.V. UPPER VOLTA, 1973-4

Table: Breakdown of cost of hand dug well programme

		Total cost per annum	Cost/ metre well $/m	% Total cost
A. Materials				
i. Cement	— 275 tonnes at $43/tonne, purchased in Abidjan, Ivory coast	11,950	6.03	8.61
	— transport 1000Km by rail, Abidjan to Ouagadougou	4,840	2.44	3.48
	— storage in Ouagadougou	110	0.06	0.09
ii. Reinforcing steel	— 30 tonnes at $442/tonne, purchased in Abidjan	13,280	6.68	9.52
	— transport 1000Km by rail, Abidjan to Ouagadougou	750	0.38	0.53
	— storage in Ouagadougou	140	0.07	0.10
	Total:	$31,070	$15.64/m	22.3%

B. Tools and Equipment

i. Hand tools	-- spades, picks, lifting tackle, pliers, crowbars etc. Amortised over 5 years, purchase cost $7,860	1,570	0.79	1.13
ii. Well shutters	— Height = 1m; Diameter = 1.40m Welded steel, 9 complete sets to each region at $300/set amortised over 10 years	2,160	1.09	1.55
iii. Donkey carts	— to carry aggregate at each well site, 10N°. at $120 each. Amortised over 5 years	240	0.12	0.17
	Total:	$3,970	$2.00/m	2.8%

C. Transport Materials & Equipment to Regional Stores

i. Hired transport	— hired carriers to haul materials from Ouagadougou to stores at regional centres	5,810	2.92	4.16
ii. Hired storage space	— storage costs at regional centres	1,560	0.79	1.13
	Total:	$7,370	$3.71/m	5.3%

D. Wages of Local Masons

— 24 masons employed during the 6 months of the year	3,080	1.55	2.21
Total:	$3,080	$1.55/m	2.2%

E. Personnel Transport between Ouagadougou & Regional Centres

i. Vehicles (6)	— Peugot 404 pick-up trucks, cost $41,000 total, amortised over 5 years	8,200	4.12	5.86
ii. Fuel	— Fuels, lubricants, servicing, spares	4,040	2.03	2.89
	Total:	$12,240	$6.15/m	8.8%

F. Administration & salaries

— Office overheads, administration costs, lodging expenses, salaries, etc. (1975 Programme costs for admin. & salaries)	81,725	41.15	58.55
Total:	$81,725	$41.15/m	58.6%

Total Programme Cost:	$139,240	$70.09/m	100.0%

CHAPTER 24   USEFUL CONTACTS

Intermediate Technology Development Group Ltd.,
103/105 Southampton Row,
London WC1B 4HH
United Kingdom

ITDG, the instigators and publishers of this manual, have a wide range of literature of many aspects of rural development. They will send a publications list on request.

International Reference Centre for Community Water Supplies,
P.O. Box 140,
Leidschendam,
Holland

This branch of the W.H.O. has been set up to act as a collection centre for the exchange of information on rural water supplies and sanitation. They issue a monthly newsheet on the activities and developments of the members in different countries and also publish collected information; they will send a publications list on request. They are producing a review of the development work on hand pumps that is being carried out by different organisations throughout the world. A report on this will be published shortly.

Volunteers in Technical Assistance,
3706 Rhode Island Avenue,
Mt. Rainier,
Maryland,
U.S.A. 20822

This organisation has a wide panel of experts who act as consultants when needed. They publish literature on all aspects of rural development; they will send a list of drawings and plans on request.

Action for Food Production,
Technical Information Service,
AFPRO, C-52,
South Extension 11,
New Delhi — 49,
India

AFPRO are a co-ordinating agency for rural development schemes in India. They publish information sheets and reports on rural water supply and sanitation and on many · other aspects of village development. Their information is concise and of great value; they will send a publications list on request.

CHAPTER 25   USEFUL SOURCES OF BASIC INFOR-
MATION ON HAND DUG WELL
CONSTRUCTION

1. *The Technique of Well Sinking in Nigeria* H.A. Cochrane.
Bulletin No. 16, Geological Survey of Nigeria 1937. 63pp.

The method of well construction described in Part II of
this manual was developed in Northern Nigeria during well
construction programmes lasting many years. The bulletin,
which is one of the most detailed and comprehensive
accounts of digging that is available, discusses in engineering
terms the factors to be considered when a well construction
programme is planned. Although it refers to experience
gained only in the geological conditions of Northern Nigeria,
the instructions and information will be of great value in
well sinking work in all parts of the world.

It includes a thorough analysis of well lining performance
and design, the amount of reinforcement and concrete that
are needed and the various cost factors for in-situ, thin
walled, reinforced concrete linings.

2. *Wells Manual -- Program and Training Journal* Action
Peace Corps, Editor Francis A. Luzzatto, Peace Corps,
Washington D.C., U.S.A. 1974. 248pp.

The U.S. Peace Corps have managed a very successful well
construction programme in West Africa for many years.
This manual is a compilation of reports and papers prepared
by the field workers who have constructed the wells.

Many detailed methods of constructing hand dug wells are
described with pictures and diagrams. It is especially useful
because it gives first-hand accounts of the problems likely to
be met in well programmes, from the organisation of supplies, the approach to successful co-operation with local
villagers, the planning of programmes and their relation-
ship to government agencies and construction techniques.

Small bore wells, hand pumps, blasting procedures are also considered in detail.

The instructions are clear and simple and the manual contains many useful hints and tips. The manual places great emphasis on the importance of considering the well programme as part of a much broader programme of development, which must include hygiene education, improved sanitation etc.

3. *The Construction and Maintenance of Water Wells* VITA Publications, College Campus, Schenectady, New York, U.S.A. 1969. 168pp.

This publication was also written for U.S. Peace Corps Volunteers who were employed to develop the ground water resources in the areas to which they were sent. It gives a general review of ground water, its occurrence and properties, well construction methods by digging, driving, drilling and jetting, well liner, boring equipment etc. It is a useful manual for field workers and is an extension to the VITA publication, 'Village Technology Handbook', first published in 1963. It has a useful section on well pumps and also on the planning aspects of a well digging programme, ground water exploration, choice of supplies, well protection and maintenance.

4. *Equipment and Techniques for the Construction of Self Help Wells* by R.G. Koegel. Annual Meeting, American Society of Agricultural Engineers. 1971.

States the general case for an appropriate technology in well construction and describes two simple well types, a small diameter augered well and a large diameter hand dug well.

Koegel emphasises the variety of techniques available for well construction and the need to improvise and adapt to suit local needs. Clearly and simply written.

5. *Well Sinking — a Working Method* by L. Lake. Gwanda, Division of Irrigation, Southern Rhodesia. 1959. 11pp.

Describes techniques developed in Rhodesia for improving indigenous well construction methods. The essential equipment included air compressors for pumping and drilling, and vehicular transportation. The air compressors allows dewatering through solid rock aquifers discharging up to 2000 litres per hour and also allows jack hammers to be used.

The advantage of using an air compressor is that there is plenty of ventilation. This method of well sinking requires fairly skilled organisation to manage the compressors, drills, explosives for blasting etc. It provides an upgraded version of hand digging needing machinery but it is not as complicated as a drilling rig — using a readily available compressor. The costs of the compressors, however, if they are not carefully maintained, can increase the costs of the wells to an unacceptable level. The notes provide very useful practical working tips on organisation, problems etc. Costs are provided with a breakdown into components.

6.   *Rural Water Development* by W.R.W. Ferguson, West African Joint Overseas Group of Engineers, Ghana Branch, March 1958.

This publication gives a general, all round description of small scale water supply systems for rural areas and compares the advantages and limitations of large diameter, hand dug wells, tubewells constructed by drilling, boring and jetting techniques etc.

Ferguson considers that the dig down — build up technique developed in Nigeria is far superior to the open caisson technique, unless the well is shallow (less than 5 metres). The caisson sinking technique is used as a telescopic tube inside the lined well when the aquifer is reached. He considers the various technical considerations to be considered before planning a programme are:—

a) Safety
b) Cost
c) Speed of construction
d) Quality of completed well
e) Mass production techniques

Small diameter boreholes are also considered in detail.

7.   *Village Wells — Their Construction, Use and Maintenance* by K.L. Hall. The Secretariat, Zomba, Nyasaland. Circular No. 12 of 1937.

A report to the Government of the time on the well construction programme between the years 1930-37. Although somewhat dated, this report gives useful information on the programme set up to construct and maintain the wells. Maintenance was regarded as a top priority and well inspectors were recruited and paid. Equipment and lubrication of the pumps, access, water levels etc. were recorded. Water samples were regularly tested and found to be of good quality despite the open well mouth. Well cleaning was part of yearly maintenance.

8. *Process Relating to Construction of Dug Wells using Homemade Casing and Hand Pumps* by R. Wieks, Mennonite Central Committee, Akron, Pennsylvania 17501, U.S.A. January 1974.

The Mennonite Society have financed well digging projects in Brazil, and these notes were written from the experience of the author.

The technique used is the caisson sinking method and the author goes into great detail on the way in which the concrete rings are made on the surface, how they are cured and lowered down the well. The mould is excessively complicated.

The second part of the paper describes how a simple piston hand pump can be constructed from commercial pipe fittings. From the evidence of other authorities, it would seem that this pump is of too weak a construction to last for long in a rural area, but the details of the piston construction are of interest.

The well cover is described. This is of RC construction. Also described are the well tripods used in construction and the pump leathers.

9. *A Safe Economical Well* American Friends Service Committee, 20 South Twelfth Street, Phil. 7, Pennsylvania, U.S.A. 1955.

A method is described which combines large diameter wells with a narrow diameter pipe making up the top section. The well is dug into the aquifer, bricks and concrete rings etc. are lowered in, the top sealed and pipes built back to the surface; the well is then back filled. A useful technique.

10. *Equipment for Radial Boring in Open Wells* by S.D. Kheper and S.K. Saudhi, Journal of Agricultural Engineering, Indian Society of Agricultural Engineers. Vol. X, No. 4. August 1973.

Describes simple equipment to drive holes into the sides of a well into the aquifer to improve well yield.

11. *Village Technology Handbook* VITA, College Campus, Schenectady, New York, U.S.A. 387pp.

This publication contains, amongst other things, information on techniques for obtaining water supplies that can be employed without expensive equipment. It contains, working drawings of tools, lists of parts needed and step by step instructions on how to do it. Techniques for drilling boreholes are given more attention than those describing hand dug wells. A useful bibliography is included.

12. *Safety in Wells and Boreholes* Institution of Civil Engineers. 1972. London. 23pp.

The handbook was written for the benefit of people engaged in well construction to inform them of the precautions that they should take to avoid accidents or the risk of contaminating the well water. The safety measures to protect the well construction are given in detail and the hazards that they could face are described. This handbook should be essential reading for anyone planning a construction programme of large diameter, hand dug wells.

13. *Concrete Practice in Building Construction* Cement and Concrete Association, 52 Grosvenor Gardens, London, United Kingdom. 66pp.

The C. & C.A. publish many 'man on the job' booklets and pamphlets on all aspects of concrete design, mixing and use. These publications are written simply with clear diagrams and photographs and will assist those who have little previous experience in concrete work. Three publications in French that set out to describe self help well construction in a similar but more technical way than that presented in this manual are listed below:—

14. *La Construction des Puits en Afrique Tropicale et 'L'Investissement Humain.'*
Ministere de la Cooperation, Paris, France. 1974.

15. *Techniques Rurales en Afrique: Hydraulique Pastorale.*
Sécretariat d'Etat aux Affaires Etrangères Chargé de la Cooperation, Paris, France.

16. *Problèmes Practiques et d'Organisation en Matière de Construction de Puits d'Eau en Grand Diametre,* 1961 René Bremand.
Provisoire du Bureau Technique, 31 Rue Marbeuf, Paris (8e), France.

On Water Pumping from Village Wells

17. *Guideline on Hand Pumps* F.E. McJunkin.

A review of W.H.O.—collaborating institutions concerning all aspects of hand pump use in rural areas. This interim report will be revised and published at a later date. One of the most complete studies to date on all aspects of hand pump use in rural areas. It reviews the main causes of failure of the pumps from the point of view of design, construction, maintenance and repair. A review of research programmes to improve various types of hand pumps is given, with information on improved designs. Guidelines for the local manufacture of hand pumps and a list of commercial manufacturers is also included. Hand dug wells are chosen in part because of the risks of pump failure in small diameter and tubewells and this publication will be of great use to organisers of well construction programmes who intend to seal their hand dug wells.

18. *Hand Pump Maintenance and the Objectives of Community Well Projects* by Arnold Pacey, to be published by OXFAM, 274 Banbury Road, Oxford, United Kingdom. 21pp.

This study considers the broader aspects of village pump maintenance and suggests that community awareness and control of the pumps are essential if they are to be kept working. The approach and objectives of the well construction programme organisers are considered thoroughly and programmes which are organised in emergencies (such as drought) are differentiated from those that aim at a larger view of development. Welfare programmes are usually short term in outlook and pump design is secondary to constructing the well. Development programmes, on the other hand, are rooted in a broader community development and choice of well type in addition to choice of pump are seen in this light. To be published at the end of 1976.

19. *The Village Tank as a Source of Drinking Water* WHO/CWS/RD/69.1 (WHO, 1211 Geneva 27, Switzerland).

A description of various low cost and simple ways to improve water supplies from the traditional village pond. It includes several examples of hand pumps suitable for local manufacture, using locally available materials.

On rural water supplies generally

20. *Water Supply for Rural Areas and Small Communities* Wagner and Lanoix, W.H.O. Monograph Series No. 42. 335pp.

A general discussion on all aspects of small scale water supply from surface and ground water sources. It includes a discussion on public health, planning and financial considerations, technical information on the various sources of water and its storage, distribution and management. It also gives diagrams and instructions on the digging, boring and jetting of wells, their lining, the pumps that can be used, development, sealing, disinfection of water supplies, etc. This is a most useful publication and is at present being reprinted by W.H.O.

21. *Small Water Supplies* Bulletin No. 10, 62pp May 1974, Ross Institute, The London School of Hygiene and Tropical Medicine, Gower Street, London WC1E 7HT, United Kingdom.

This publication is one of a series of practical and simple guides to health and hygiene in tropical countries. It gives a basic description of the requirements of a wholesome water supply, the alternative sources, their collection and treatment. An excellent practical guide for rural workers.

22. *Water Resources Development* A.F.P.R.O. publication N29, 1969, C-52, South Extension, New Delhi, India. 138pp.

The papers from A.F.P.R.O conference on water resources development held in 1969 are contained in this publication. It contains many useful articles describing the experience gained in well digging and boring in India, including geophysical exploration, geological mapping and boreholes, well re-vitalisation. A.F.P.R.O. is a co-ordinating body on village development and distributes a great deal of information in the form of short leaflets available on request.

23. *Rural Water Supply & Sanitation in Less-Developed Countries*. A selected annotated bibliography by Anne U. White and Chris Sevior. From IDRC Box 8500, Ottowa, Canada K1G 3H9 $1.00. 1974. 81pp.

One of the most comprehensive bibliographies available on rural water supplies and sanitation. It describes the most important publications on all aspects of the subject, that are both readily available or that only exist as unpublished internal reports within research organisations etc. This is an essential source for locating further information.

24. *Drawers of Water* White, Bradley, White, University of Chicago Press. 1972. 306pp.

This book describes the results of a detailed study of water use in rural and town areas of East Africa, giving details of the domestic consumption of water, the choices made between alternative sources, the distance water is carried, etc. It gives a critical evaluation of the relationships between water quality and quantity and the health of the water users.

This is a truly excellent book for those who wish to gain a broad understanding of water supplies and their relation to the users. It also gives a general idea of the costs of obtaining a water supply from different sources.

25. *Water Treatment and Sanitation* I.T.D.G. Publications, 9 King Street, London WC2E 8HN, United Kingdom. 1973. 90pp. (Revised edition 1976).

A description of low cost methods of obtaining water supplies and of effluent disposal. It includes worked examples of basic design methods and is directed mainly towards the needs of small communities. It describes a wide range of techniques, giving a general comparison between them.

26. *Small Wells Manual: A Manual of Location, Design, Construction, Use and Maintenance* Gibson and Singer. Health Service, Office of War on Hunger, A.I.D. Washington DC 20523. 1969. 156pp.

This manual has been written as a basic introduction to well boring and drilling for those with little personal experience on the subject. It is mainly concerned with small tube wells of up to 10cms in diameter, with maximum depth of 30 metres and with yields of up to 200 litre/minute. It considers bored, driven, jetted and drilled tube wells but does not include hand dug wells; it treats the subject simply and contains a useful bibliography. This publication gives a short and concise description of ground water, its origin, occurrence and movement, and a useful section on ground water exploration.

On rural sanitation

27. *Excreta Disposal for Rural Areas and Small Communites* E.G. Wagner and J.N. Lanoix, W.H.O., Geneva, Monograph Series No. 39. 1958. 187pp.

A companion volume to the publication on rural water supplies, this is a basic reference for rural sanitation workers.

It describes the health hazards of poor sanitation, the necessity of involving the local people in the improvement of their hygiene standards and a description of the various simple ways available for rural communities. It is addressed primarily to those who are responsible for the organisation of public health programmes.

28. *Rural Sanitation in the Tropics* Ross Institute, The London School of Hygiene and Tropical Medicine, Gower Street, London WC1E 7HT. Bulletin No. 8, May 1974. 46pp.

A basic description of the various ways that family privies and public latrines can be constructed and maintained. Dimensioned diagrams are provided with the advantages and limitations of each technique. Sections are included on larger scale effluent disposal, latrine maintenance and waste stabilisation ponds.

APPENDIX THE USE OF EXPLOSIVES IN WELL-SINKING WORK

Summary

This chapter has been prepared as a supplement to the original edition of this book. It is intended to describe the use of explosives for sinking large diameter wells through hard rocks.

It is intended only as a practical guide to those already experienced and qualified in the use of explosives, and to demonstrate the potential of rock blasting for wells. *It will not serve to qualify an inexperienced man in rock blasting work.*

The supplement describes the various methods of using explosives in well-sinking work, and recommends that the burning fuse type of detonation be used because of its simplicity and foolproof nature. Electric detonation is described as well as the safety rules that must be observed if accidents are to be avoided.

1. Sinking through hard rocks

The geological strata that cause the greatest number of wells to be abandoned by traditional well diggers before they reach water are hard, solid rocks that can only be broken by laborious and exhaustive effort. At this stage, the well digger should seriously consider abandoning the well and moving to a new, more likely site. But if the rock formation is known to contain water in its fissures, then it can be penetrated by blasting and excavation.

It is possible, of course, to penetrate most formations other than solid basement rock by the use of sledge hammers and chisels. Even bedrocks such as granite have been tackled by local well sinkers by the traditional

235

method of lighting fires on the exposed surface of the rocks and, when the material is sufficiently heated, pouring on cold water in large quantities. The violent contraction of the surface which results causes cracks to the depth of several centimetres and this cracked layer can then be broken off with a pick or crowbar. Apart from the difficulties of this method — not the least of which is to obtain sufficient heat from a fire at the bottom of an unventilated shaft — it is laborious and slow in the extreme. As a practical operation it is, in fact, obsolete and is only quoted here to show the ingenuity with which the traditional well builders overcame conditions (which must at first have appeared to them impossible) with the equipment at their disposal.

Compressed-air tools are also widely used in well programmes to break up hard rocks. However, these need an expensive air compressor that must be serviced, maintained, and taken to the well sites which are often in difficult terrain. One advantage of using compressed-air tools is the possibility of pumping the well dry with an air-powered pump during sinking. This allows the well to be sunk deep into the aquifer.

Explosives make a very valuable tool for well sinking through hard rocks, and if blasting skills and qualifications are available these will speed up the rate of sinking considerably. The use of explosives in well-sinking work is described in greater detail below.

2. Rules and regulations covering the use of explosives

In most countries of the world explosives can only be used by those people who have been issued with blasting certificates; these are issued only when trainees have shown their experience and responsibility in the use of explosives. It is usually an offence for unqualified and unrecognised people to use explosives.

Strict laws are enforced about the rules and procedures to be adopted in the purchase, transportation, storage, and use of explosives. These rules and procedures are not within the scope of this publication, and enquiries

must be made from the appropriate government department or police authority in your area.

Explosives are costly and in inexperienced hands very
dangerous to use. They should only be employed when
there is no other way of sinking through the hard rocks.
They need very careful attention and supervision if
serious or fatal accidents are to be avoided. The rules
and regulations covering their use have been drawn up
by experts for the safety of both those using the explosives
and the general public — these rules and regulations
must be rigidly adhered to.

3. Types of explosives, detonators, and accessory equipment

a) *Explosives*. Rock blasting with explosives is carried
out by the massive hammer blow of the rapidly expand-
gases from the explosives which have been drilled into
and detonated within the rocks.

There are many different types of explosive manufactured today, each of which has its own uses, but the
types found to be particularly adaptable to well sinking
are gelignite or one of the blasting gelatines. These
consist of mixtures of nitro-glycerine and other ingredients: briefly it may be said that the nitro-glycerine
gives the explosive power and the other ingredients are
added to make the explosive safer to handle, convenient
to use and less likely to deteriorate in storage.

Expert help must be sought in selecting the most
suitable explosive for well-blasting work. It should be
safe to handle, waterproof (fire under water), malleable
enough to squeeze into cracks and drill holes, and
produce gases on firing that are non-toxic.

Many commercially available gelignites are suitable,
and they are usually supplied in 25kg boxes, in waxed
paper cartridges 25mm in diameter and 100 or 200mm in
length.

b) *Detonators*. Gelignite and similar compounds do not
explode when they are ignited, they will just burn
furiously. In order to start the explosion, a sudden blow
is necessary, which is one reason why the material has

to be handled so carefully. A blow from a hammer or similar tool will detonate the explosive material, although it is obviously not possible to do this with safety.

Detonators are therefore used to start the explosion — they consist of a small quantity of a different type of explosive called 'fulminate', sealed into the end of a hollow metal tube about 50mm long and 6mm in diameter. When the detonator is inserted into the explosive and fired, a small explosion takes place, and the shock of this is enough to propagate an explosion through the main body of the gelignite. The detonators are fired either by an electrical trigger, or a burning safety fuse.

The electrically fired detonators have an electric heating device sealed into the fulminate. An electric current is passed into the detonator through two insulated wires which are attached to a firing cable running down into the well from the surface. An electric current is passed down the firing cable from an 'exploder' — powered either by a battery or a small hand-operated generator, to detonate the explosives.

The detonators are made to fire either instantaneously

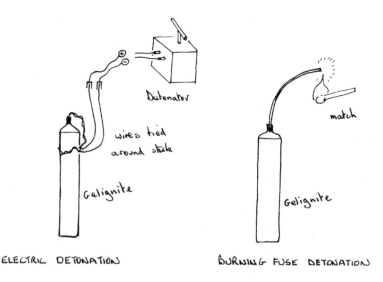

ELECTRIC DETONATION   BURNING FUSE DETONATION

Fig. 1   Detonation of charges.

with the passage of the current, or at delayed intervals of from 0 to 12 seconds. Extreme safety precautions must be taken with electric detonators to avoid the risk of accidental firing by stray electric currents.

Burning fuse detonators are fired by the heat of a waterproof burning fuse, which is ignited and burns its way down to the fulminate. The fuse is ignited from the surface, and because the fuse cannot readily be ignited by accident, and because the process of burning can be readily seen, this type of detonation is recommended as the safest and most foolproof.

Both gelignite and detonators have an expiration date stamped on the cases. Do not use an old batch as it may be inherently unstable and dangerous.

c) *Accessory equipment*
  i. For electric shot firing the following equipment will be needed:
    Exploder — battery or hand generator-powered condenser to produce the electric charge.
    Ohmeter — an instrument to test the electric circuit in case of misfires.
    Shot-firing cable — a well-insulated, two core cable, about 100 metres long, each core consisting of at least four copper wires of not less than 0.46mm diameter.
    Steining rods, scraper, etc. — for loading the charges.
  ii. For burning fuse shot-firing, the following equipment is needed:
    Burning fuse — suitable lengths of dry, waterproof burning fuse, with the correct detonators.
    Ignition equipment — thin wire, about 50m long, down which a burning rag slides to ignite the fuse at the bottom of the well.

4. Rock blasting using burning fuse type detonators

The method of shot firing using burning fuse detonators described in this section has been developed from extensive field experience in rural areas. The risks of accidental detonation are reduced to a minimum, and the method is almost foolproof.

4.1 Drilling the shot holes

The practical effect of the explosion from a detonated charge is to deliver an extremely powerful 'hammer blow' in all directions simultaneously. Consequently, if a stick of gelignite is detonated on the surface of hard rock the greater part of the power produced will be wasted in the air, and only slight damage will be done to the material below. For this reason, in order to utilise the explosive force to its fullest extent, the charge must be exploded down shot-holes within the rock, so that the shock and the expansion produced by the explosion will lift the material above and shatter the rock around the charge.

It is usual in a 1.30 metre diameter well to lay three charges at one time. These charges are set in the form of an equilateral triangle with each rather more than 30 centimetres from the side of the hole. In granite each charge is set about 1 metre below the surface — with this arrangement it is found that the shattering effect of the explosions covers the whole of the bottom of the well without wasting any appreciable part of the energy outside the area required to be broken up.

The first operation, therefore, is to drill three holes in this pattern in the well bottom. In remote areas it is not usually practicable to use compressed air tools which are, of course, much more easy and quick than hand tools. Instead it is usual to use a sledge hammer and jumper bar. The sledge hammer should be about 2 kg in weight with a handle not longer than $\frac{1}{2}$ metre, this being the largest size which can conveniently be wielded at the well bottom. The jumper bar is a long cold chisel made from 25mm hexagonal section tool steel with the chisel edge approximately 30mm across. The shape of the section and the very slightly wider point prevent the bar from jamming in the hole. One man holds the bar vertically in position and rotates it slightly between each blow delivered by the second man. It is usual to have a number of bars varying in length between about $\frac{1}{2}$ and

1½ metres so that the head of the bar can always be in a convenient striking position as the hole goes deeper into the rock:

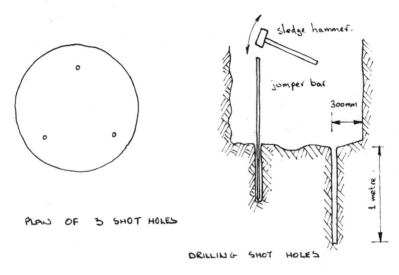

PLAN OF 3 SHOT HOLES

DRILLING SHOT HOLES

Fig. 2   Drilling shot holes by hand.

4.2 Loading the shot holes and preparing the vertical wire

When the shot holes have been drilled to the required depth, they are cleaned out, and 'charged' with the explosives; the quantity of gelignite used depends on the type of rock and the depth of the drilled hole, but with 1 metre deep holes in reasonably hard rock it is usual to put four 100mm sticks into each. Gelignite sticks are inserted one at a time without removing the oiled paper covering, and each is pressed firmly into the hole by a *wooden* stick of a diameter slightly less than that of the hole. *A metal rod should never be used* nor should undue force or a sudden blow. The mouth of the hole should then be protected with a twist of paper or wooden plug against stone fragments falling in above the charge.

The next step is to fix a vertical wire near the side of the well from the surface to the bottom. Reinforcing tie wire pulled straight is normally used for this purpose, the lower end fastened to a heavy stone and the top fixed to the well headframe. It should be about 15cm from the side of the well so that it is not fouled by the operator when he is pulled up after laying the charges.

4.3 Preparing the detonators and the priming charges

The safety fuse (burning fuse) is now inserted into the detonators. This operation is carried out on the surface, and is one of the last things to be done before the detonators are fitted into the top sticks of gelignite — the priming charge — ready for firing the charged shot holes.

Safety fuse is obtained in rolls, and consists of a cord about 5mm in diameter composed of an even-burning core surrounded with a protective waterproof coat and strengthened outside with a sheath of fibre. It burns at a predetermined rate, usually thirty seconds per 30cm, and for well-blasting work should always be of the best waterproof quality which will stand immersion and burn equally well above or below water. When charges are prepared the exact length of fuse required is accurately measured and cut off the roll with a square end by a sharp knife. The square cut is most important — a diagonal cut should never be used.

No. 6 type detonators for use with safety fuse are used and are supplied in metal boxes of 100 each. Detonators must be handled extremely carefully as excessive heat or scratch or a blow can set off an explosion. They are usually packed with powdered cork and the first thing to do on removing a detonator from its box is to ensure that no cork particle remains in the hollow end as such a particle could cause a misfire. If any packing or dust is to be removed from the inside of the tube it may be blown out, but on no account should a stick, wire or anything else be poked into the tube end to clean it.

When a fuse has been cut to the required length, one end is inserted into the hollow end of the detonator and the thin metal 'crimped' on to the fuse by means of special crimping pliers. A practice which must be most expressly forbidden is the extremely dangerous one of biting the detonator on to the fuse with the teeth. This can result in serious or fatal injury if the detonator accidentally explodes.

The detonator and fuse end are now inserted into a stick

of gelignite. The high explosive itself is a sticky brown substance rather like solidified honey, and is supplied in 'sticks' of about 25mm in diameter and 100-200mm in length. Each stick comes wrapped in tough oiled brown paper, usually with fifty sticks packed into a waxed cardboard cylindrical carton of about 5kg in weight. One stick is taken, the oiled paper unfolded at one end and with a *wooden* rod about the size of a pencil an axial hole is made for about half the length of the stick. Into this is pushed the detonator and fuse end, the gelignite is squeezed around the fuse to prevent any water seeping between the explosive and fuse, and a short length of adhesive tape bound round the point where the fuse enters the paper cover. The stick is now said to be 'primed' and is referred to as a 'priming cartridge'. Great care must now be taken with the primed cartridge in order to avoid an accidental explosion.

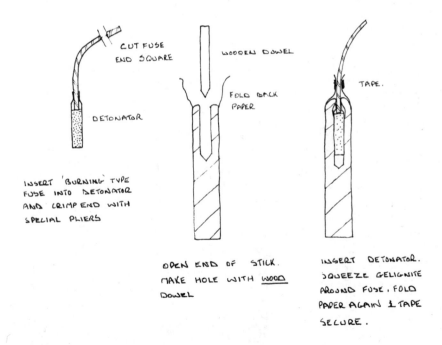

Fig. 3   *Preparing priming charge.*

4.4 Loading the priming charges into the shot holes

Now the priming cartridges are prepared with the important proviso that the fuse of the three shall be of different lengths, 1.30, 1.45 and 1.60 metres being convenient sizes to allow the charges to be fired one after another at about 15 second intervals. They are taken down the well and one cartridge lowered carefully into each hole on to the surface of the gelignite already packed in place. While it is important that the priming cartridge should be in direct contact with the main charge no stick or other instrument should be used to push it into place.

The free ends of the three fuses are bound together and to the vertical wire about 30cm above the well bottom with string or adhesive tape. One stick of gelignite without a detonator is then removed from its paper wrapping and the three fuse ends pressed into this gelignite which should then be tied against the wire.

If the well is dry it will now be necessary to fill the charged holes to the surface with water without disturb-

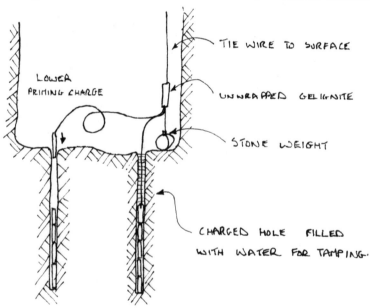

Fig. 4 Charging shot holes.

ing the priming cartridges or fuses in so doing. Frequently the well is not dry owing to slight seepages of water through the well sides above the rock : in this case there will already be sufficent water 'tamping', the purpose of which is to communicate the explosion shock evenly throughout the hole (water being virtually incompressible) and also to prevent the expansion force of the explosion gases being uselessly blown out of the open hole. It is not necessary to use sand, clay or other tamping. Not only is water just as effective, provided that there is a column of at least 30cm depth above the priming cartridge, but should there be for any reason a misfire, a second priming cartridge can be put down later without disturbing the first, and the long, laborious and possibly dangerous operation of dealing with a misfire in a sealed hole is avoided.

4.5 Firing the charges

The well is now ready for firing, and the operator in charge of the blasting is lifted out the well and ensures that, except for the headframe, nothing is immediately around the well mouth, and everyone except himself has withdrawn to a safe distance. He then takes a piece of rag soaked in petrol or kerosene, ties it loosely round the vertical wire, lights it and allows it to slide freely down the wire. He watches it reach the point where the fuses are tied, and when the rag reaches the unwrapped gelignite the latter will burst into flame and will simultaneously ignite all three fuses. After that the operator himself retires from the well mouth and waits for the three explosions, which, if the fuses have been cut to the lengths suggested above, will occur at 15 second intervals following the first, which will take place about two minutes after the fuses have lit.

Some operators adopt a further precaution against a misfire. Before inserting the priming cartridges the end of a length of thin copper wire is wound round each. The opposite ends of these copper wires are now fastened to the lower end of the vertical wire down which the petrol rag slides. On the explosion this wire binding is disintegrated at the cartridge end, but should a misfire for any reason occur the cartridge concerned can be lifted out of the hole complete with detonator and fuse, without the necessity of descending the well, provided that water tamping has been used as described. This is an important reason for using water as a tamping material in the shot holes.

Apart from the drilling of the shot holes in the rock, the work of laying and preparing the charges will normally have taken about half an hour. Because of the fumes released by the explosion, which are dangerous to breathe in a confined space, it is usual to make blasting operations the last job in a working day — by next morning the fumes will have dispersed. However, should it be necessary to descend after the explosions the air may be cleared to a great extent by sprinkling sand or water down one side of the well to induce an air current, by winding a sinking kibble rapidly up and down the well a few times, or, if a ventilation fan is available, a few minutes blowing will suffice.

4.6 Advantages of burning fuse detonation

One advantage of the safety fuse method just described is that the three explosions occur separately and can (and must) be counted individually. With electric detonation the explosions are usually simultaneous (unless different time fuses are used) and without descending the well and inspecting it is impossible to be certain that all three have gone off. The danger to workmen descending to clear the loosened rock with an unexploded charge remaining in position is too obvious to enlarge upon. A second advantage is that the requirements are simple — gelignite, detonators, fuse and binding wire — while the electric method requires, in addition, firing cable (which is frequently damaged by rock fragments from the explosion and consequently needs constant renewing) the exploder itself which, while robust, is by no means indestructible, and a delicate milliammeter for testing the circuit before firing. In addition the electrical operator needs more skill and experience in view of the additional invisible electronic 'snags' which can occur.

4.7 Removing the loosened rock

After the explosion and the clearing of the atmosphere in the well the loosened rock is removed by hand and the new bottom trimmed with picks and miners' bars ready for the drilling of the next three shot holes. These should be sited clear of any fissures which may have developed below the well bottom due to blasting. Sometimes it will be found that the last few inches of the previously drilled holes are still visible on the new rock face owing to the gelignite not having been pressed right home, or to a stone or dirt having got into the hole before charging. *On no account, and this is extremely important, should drilling of new holes be started in these old holes.* The temptation for the well diggers to save a few centimetres rock drilling is considerable, but experience has shown that the accidents which occasionally happen in well blasting work have been through drilling in an old hole, into which a small fragment of unexploded gelignite had squeezed from a previous blast.

4.8 Safety procedures

The safety procedures which must be adopted and rigidly adhered to are described in greater detail in Section 6. Certain precautions are so obvious that they should not need mentioning; but the very fact of their being obvious means that they are occasionally overlooked. Operators have been found smoking when handling explosives; gelignite and detonators have been found stored in the same box; unused gelignite which should have been returned to the magazine has been found lying about where a chance blow could start an explosion; metal rods which can strike a spark from rock have been used instead of wooden tampers, etc. All these things are a matter of common sense and it is essential that persons handling explosive materials should have a well-developed sense of responsibility and a thorough knowledge of and respect for the materials they are handling.

Another point to note is that the nitro-glycerine contained in gelignite is a poison, and one that can be absorbed through the skin. If handled too much it can cause severe headaches and sickness. This possibility is minimized by wearing rubber gloves or keeping the hands constantly wet while handling the sticks; a pan of water into which the hands are frequently dipped will be found by the side of all experienced blasters. Care must also be taken against breathing any of the fumes after the explosion or the same symptoms will result.

With proper precautions, blasting is simple, straight-forward and safe, but there is no short cut and no sensible man will wish to risk his own and other lives for the want of a little trouble.

5. Rock blasting using electrical detonators

Electrical detonators have already been described in Section 3b and the dangers of accidental firing have been stressed. However, the electrical method has the advantage of speed, and may be used with benefit when a large programme of blasting is taking place in a small district; but for single wells in remote areas the safety fuse method will be found to be safer and more con-venient every time.

The procedure for blasting using the electric type detonators, and the precautions to be taken, are exactly similar to the procedure described above for burning fuse detonation, except for the firing arrangement.

5.1 Wiring up the electric detonators

The shot holes are drilled and loaded with gelignite. The detonators with different time fuses are selected, loaded into the priming charge, sealed with tape and loaded into the shot holes. The leads from the detonators should be wired up in parallel; that is, the two leads of different colours from each detonator should be joined in separate knots above the water.

This method does not eliminate misfires due to dud detonators, but the incidence of duds is very rare, and usually the presence of a misfired shot hole can readily be seen by the coloured tags on the detonator leads. When wired in series, a dud detonator will break the circuit and prevent firing altogether, but the dud must

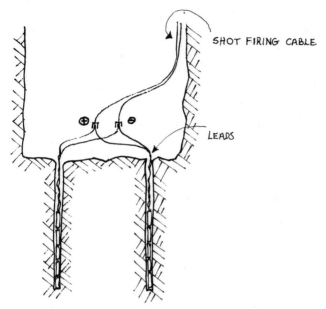

SHOT FIRING CABLE

LEADS

Fig. 5   Connecting electric leads to shot-firing cable.

then be located with the ohmeter, which is a highly dangerous operation even for the experienced.

5.2 Firing the charges by the exploder

Before the knots of detonator leads are connected to the shot firing cable, make sure that the exploder key, or batteries, are with you, and that someone is guarding the exploder and cable.

Finally, connect the detonator leads to the shot firing cable, climb out of the well, check that the well head is clear, and fire the charges by operating the exploder. Count the explosions, and give the well time to clear of noxious gases before the well diggers descend to clear away rubble.

At the end of each blasting operation, check that the cable is not severed or damaged, using the ohmeter and batteries ; the cable will then be ready for use at the next firing.

5.3 Procedure in case of misfires

Pull up the cable and count the number of detonator leads; if all the shot holes have fired, then there will be the same number of loose leads, but if the cable is held fast, then there is a chance of a misfire.

Wait for half an hour or so until the smoke and fumes have cleared, before you climb down into the well and check the detonator leads. If you see a set of leads running into the shattered rock, disconnect the detonator leads from the shot firing cable, dig carefully into the rubble, and pull the detonator out slowly. You must fire this charged shot hole before digging recommences, or a blow from a shovel or pick axe may set it off. Set a new detonator in the gelignite and fire this; if the shot still does not fire, put a new stick of gelignite into the top of the shot hole and fire again.

6. Standing safety rules with explosives

Storage
- Store in a safe, dry fireproof place.
- Do not smoke near explosives.
- Never store gelignite and detonators in the same box.
- Do not use metal tools to open boxes full of explosives.
- Keep a careful check in writing on the amount of explosives used.
- Do not use damaged or deteriorated explosives.
- Do not store in your home.
- Try to arrange storage with local police.

Transportation
- Carry in a proper container.
- Never carry the gelignite and detonators in the same box.
- Only carry the amount you need for blasting.
- Handling the gelignite with wet hands reduces the risks of poisoning.

Loading the Charges
- Do not soften gelignite by heating.
- Do not force cartridge into the shot holes.

- Use water to stem the shot hole.
- Do not use a metal rod to stem shot hole, use a wooden one.
- Do not use more charge than you have to.

Electric Detonators

- Do not force detonators into charges.
- Straighten electric detonator leads carefully and hitch around charge with waterproof tape.
- Do not allow leads to touch metal rods, pipes, etc., especially near electrical equipment.
- Hold leads to side of shot hole to avoid stripping with stemming rod.
- Connect detonators in parallel by knotting leads of same colour.
- Keep knots above water and to side of well.
- Keep electric detonator leads short circuited until connection is needed with firing cable, by connecting the knots.
- Do not connect detonator leads to shot-firing cable until you are ready for firing.
- *Keep the exploder key or batteries with you.*

The Shot-firing Cable

- Testing the electric shot-firing cable for breaks before it is connected to the detonators.
- Keep bare ends of shot-firing cable at surface short circuited until connection is required to exploder.
- Keep firing circuit insulated from ground, soils, wires, pipes, etc., to avoid picking up stray electrical currents.
- Clean connectors with detonator leads thoroughly to avoid poor contacts and misfires.
- Use waterproof insulating tape around knots.

The Exploder	● Keep all keys and batteries safely with you when you are down the well.
	● Connect shot-firing cable only when you are ready to fire.
	● Keep exploder in a dry place, and test at intervals.
Burning Fuse Detonators	● Load carefully into priming charge.
	● Cut fuse carefully with a knife to make a square end.
	● Do not clean detonator out with wire or a stick, blow it clean.
	● Do not crimp detonator around fuse with your teeth.
	● Make sure that detonator is firmly imbedded in priming charge, then seal brown paper with waterproof tape.
	● (It will be seen that burning fuse detonators are very much more simple to handle than electric detonators.)
Firing	● Check that all people are clear of the well before firing.
	● Do not enter well for at least 2 hours.
	● Do not blast during electrical storms.
Misfires with Electrical Detonators	● Disconnect exploder, short cut cable.
	● Take out batteries and key.
	● Go down the well yourself to check for dead charges.

The well-blaster must consider himself (or herself) responsible for each and every stage of the blasting operation — he/she must not delegate responsibility to his/her workmen.

7. Where to go for further information

Commercial Literature

7.1. *Blasting Practice,* Imperial Chemical Industries Ltd., Nobel Division, Stevenston, Ayrshire, Scotland, U.K.

7.2. *Blasters Handbook,* E. I. Dupont Nemours, Wilmington, Delaware, U.S.A. Price $6.00 approx.

These publications have been written for professional workers with explosives. They are comprehensive and give detailed accounts of all aspects of explosive use.

A Description of Explosives used in Well Sinking

7.3. *Wells Manual — Programme & Training Journal,* Action Peace Corps, 1974. 248 pp.

The U.S. Peace Corps have managed a very successful well-construction programme in West Africa for many years. This manual is a compilation of reports and papers prepared by the field workers who have constructed the wells.

Many methods of well construction are described in detail, including an account of the use of electric-detonated blasting for deepening large diameter wells through hard rocks.

7.4. *Water Resources Development,* AFPRO Publication N. 29. 1969, C-52, South Extension, New Delhi, India. 138 pp.

Action for Food Production is a co-ordinating body on village development in India. It organised a successful conference on water resources development in New Delhi in 1969, and the papers from this conference have been collected together for this publication. Several of the papers give detailed accounts of well-blasting procedures and the regulations in force in India governing their use.